BETSY SCHOW

FINISHED
being
FAT

AN ACCIDENTAL ADVENTURE
in **LOSING WEIGHT** *and*
LEARNING HOW *to* **FINISH**

WITHDRAWN

PLAIN SIGHT PUBLISHING

AN IMPRINT OF CEDAR FORT, INC
SPRINGVILLE, UTAH

TO JAROM, CALEB, AND MY DAD. THIS BOOK WOULDN'T EXIST WITHOUT YOU.

ISBN 13:978-1-4621-1125-1

Published by Plain Sight Publishing, an imprint of Cedar Fort, Inc.
2373 W. 700 S., Springville, UT 84663

Distributed by Cedar Fort, Inc., www.cedarfort.com

LIBRARY OF CONGRESS CATALOGING-IN-PUBLICATION DATA

Schow, Betsy, 1981- author.
  Finished being fat / Betsy Schow.
    pages cm
  Includes bibliographical references and index.
  Summary: Suggestions, tips, and ideas on how to finish what you start.
  ISBN 978-1-4621-1125-1 (alk. paper)
  1. Self-confidence. 2. Weight loss. 3. Self-acceptance in women. I. Title.

  BJ1533.S27S36 2013
  158.1--dc23

                      2012042440

Cover design by Erica Dixon
Cover design © 2013 by Lyle Mortimer
Edited and typeset by Whitney A. Lindsley

Printed in the United States of America

10 9 8 7 6 5 4 3 2 1

"Not only is *Finished Being Fat* engaging and relevant to every woman that has ever had a sliver of self doubt about her body, but your true "voice" and your self-effacing humor make you the sister that has walked the walk right along with me. I recognize my own internal critic in your story. It is compelling. I found myself sneaking back to my computer while the kids ate their Cheerios, or late at night to read another dozen pages. I could not stop. You bravely share the paradigms of your pre-thin mind-set and include the reader on a journey as you become enlightened as to your own worth and power. You are so clearly priceless, and because you pull us along with you via hilarious anecdotal "aha" moments, we recognize this truth about ourselves right along with you. This book is for EVERYONE, whether or not they have battled weight. It ultimately inspires us to keep on running, never give up, and finish."

—**Tres Hatch,** TV chef and author of *Miracle Pill: 10 Truths to Healthy, Thin, and Sexy*

This book is bright and inspiring—and best of all, doable. Finished Being Fat is the next "Eat, Pray, Love." You will fall in love with Betsy's charming, honest voice—and then you will fall in love with yourself, all over again.

—**Caleb Warnock,** bestselling author of *Forgotten Skills*

"**Proof that losing** weight can be funny, too. Betsy is open and honest—a welcome voice in the discussion about body image and getting fit."

—FitBottomedGirls.com

"**Not only an entertaining** read in its own right, but *Finished Being Fat* is full of common sense approaches to a happier and healthier life. I would definitely recommend it to anyone struggling to reach their goals and overcome the burdens of past failures.

—Jeffry H. Larson, PhD, bestselling author of *Should We Stay Together*

"**I loved this** book from beginning to end. Betsy has a natural sense of humor and down-to-earth way of looking at the world and weight loss, and I appreciated her honesty about her feelings and trials. *Finished Being Fat* inspired me, and I know it will inspire you, too."

—Tristi Pinkston, author of *The Secret Sisters Mysteries* and others

"*Finished Being Fat* is an engaging true story about one woman's battle with herself. In her journey to lose weight, Betsy learns her problems are deeper than dropping pounds. She learns to drop the walls and attitudes that keep her from living the life she deserves. The epiphanies within this book truly do inspire others to break out of their self-imposed walls and go on their own journeys."

—Nikki Wilson, founder of MormonMommyWriters.blogspot.com

CONTENTS

CONTENTS

ACKNOWLEDGMENTS

There would be no story without the support of the Fat Pack: Chris Dalley, Sarah Michelle Croxford, Susan Eisert, Mallory Lambson, Lori Chadwick, Sharon Kono, Star Monson, and honorary members, Misty Barry and Lacey Hammond. Not to mention my running partner, Chrisy Ross. You ladies rock, and you kept me going. You are all beautiful and amazing, and I am blessed to have you in my corner.

My family deserves major props for putting up with all my nuttiness. Read the book, and you'll understand. Foremost, my husband Jarom, for loving me and supporting my dreams at any size. My parents were absolutely invaluable during marathon training so I didn't have to push an eighty-pound stroller for twenty miles. And Leslie and Kiara Schow for their love and babysitting services while I wrote the book. And my sisters, Jaime, Stacey, Jill, and Kristine, for being you. Even when you taunted me with cookies.

A big thank-you to Sunshine Academy for helping with the girls on the long runs. And Characa Waters and Mandi Edgerly for your extra support and understanding while I worked with Lily during the rough times.

Thank you to everyone at Cedar Fort for you hard work to make my dream a reality. Angie Workman and Whitney Lindsley are the best editors on the planet. They deserves untold fortunes for putting up with authors like me.

I owe my writing style and success to my two writing groups. Karen Pellet, TJ Bronley, Jessica Guernsey, Julie Peterson, Stacy Kupiec, Elaine Hume, Melody Johnson, Tanya Hanamaikai, Vickie Erickson, Kari Pike,

ACKNOWLEDGMENTS

and Jenny Alvear—thanks for telling me when my writing sucked and when it worked.

Last but never least, my undying gratitude to Caleb Warnock, writing professor extraordinaire. When I showed up at your conference one day, I had a little twinkle of an idea that you convinced me just might be a book. Even more than that, you believed there might be a writer lurking somewhere. The way you can shape and mold an author is a rare and exquisite talent. You pushed me harder than any marathon and never let me give up. You shaped this book and provided valuable insight into who I've become and where I am going in life. Your friendship is one of my most prized finisher medals.

INTRODUCTION

This is not a weight-loss book. If you bought this book because you wanted to learn the secret to losing seventy-five pounds in a year, then let me stop you right here. There's no magic pill—just eat less and run more.

This is also not a book about how to run a marathon, even though I include lot of stories about running.

Nope, this book is all about the things I learned while I was losing weight and running that changed my life forever. I've taken all my little "duh" moments—when the lightbulb finally turns on in my brain—and found little inspirational cubbyholes to put them in—otherwise known as chapters.

I'm not a doctor, motivational speaker, elite athlete, or anything in between. My name is Betsy Schow, and I'm just a stay-at-home mom of two, former fat person, marathoner, mountain climber, and finisher. I didn't set out to change my life, but like some of the best things, it kind of happened by accident. At first, all I wanted was to lose a few pounds so I could look in the mirror and not cringe. The other things I just figured out on the way when I started paying attention.

The process started with the sound that often accompanies the moment when you know your life has somehow gone awry . . .

YOU'LL KNOW YOU'VE HIT *the* BOTTOM WHEN YOU HEAR *the* THUD

Daily routine: Wake up, feed kids, entertain kids, keep kids from killing each other, put kids to bed, put kids back to bed thirty minutes later, and then collapse into my own bed and fade into unconsciousness. Repeat.

My life was a lot like running on a treadmill, a whole lot of effort to get absolutely nowhere. Not that I had much experience with treadmills, mind you, but you get my drift. One morning, I woke up depressed and berated myself for all the things that I wasn't. Wasn't skinny, wasn't accomplished, wasn't happy. In a fit of masochism, I decided it would be a good time to take on my mortal enemy, the digital scale.

The scale and I have always had a hate/more hate relationship. I've tried sweet talking it, I've tried yelling at it, and I've even tried approaching it with cautious optimism. Power of positive thinking and all. Recently, I had given it the silent treatment, refusing to acknowledge its existence. But apparently I felt the need to punish myself, because there I was again, at seven in the morning, before the children were awake, naked and oh-so-carefully avoiding the adjacent mirror (because let's be honest, who wants to see themselves naked first thing in the morning?) and ever so lightly (because it might make a difference) stepping on the scale. While I waited for the scale to stop blinking 0.00 and pronounce judgment, I began to pray.

"Please, God. Just let it be the same as last month. I'm not asking for it be lower, just . . . please, let it be the same." God was apparently out of miracles. The scale read 216.4 pounds—ten pounds more than the last month. I looked around just to be sure my fourteen-month-old hadn't sneaked up behind me, adding her sixteen pounds to the total. Nope, I was alone. So I hopped off and tried again, just in case. Maybe the scale had changed its mind, had a technical error, or something. But no, the evil scale seemed to take joy in my misery and now said 216.6. *Ahhhh!* I had gained a fifth of a pound in less than a minute.

Scenes from my future played out in my mind. I would gain a pound every hour. Within a week, none of my clothes would fit. By the end of the month, I would have to order everything from an online specialty store, Blobbos. In a year, my husband would need to physically roll me out of the bed and onto a Jazzy scooter because I had gotten so big that my legs wouldn't support my girth. I was going to be like that woman from *What's Eating Gilbert Grape.* When I died, they would have to cut a hole in my house just to get me out. Then I'd have to be buried in a packing crate because surely no one would make a coffin large enough to fit me.

I backpedaled off the scale so fast that I tripped. That's when I heard the *thud* of my life hitting rock bottom. It was so loud it even woke my husband, Jarom. Well, it was either that or the crash from the scale reverberating off the travertine. I imagine he ran into the bathroom, expecting to find that I had slipped in the shower. He probably did not expect to see his naked, overweight wife sprawled on the floor, trying to beat the scale into submission.

"Betsy, what the heck are you doing?"

"I'm fat!" I wailed

My husband, always a man of few words, wisely said nothing and offered me a hand up. For a few minutes, we stood there, him patting my back and me sobbing onto his shoulder. After I had quieted down some, Jarom grabbed a pack of tissues and herded me back into the bedroom. He sat me down on the bed and wiped the tears and snot off my face, then did the same for his shoulder.

"Now start over and tell me what's wrong."

There weren't enough hours in the day or words in the English language to describe what was wrong. At that moment, I felt like the most worthless human being on the planet. Every disappointment, every failure echoed in stereo through my head. It was too overwhelming to think about, so I tried to focus on the immediate problem of my weight.

"Somehow I gained ten pounds this month." I sniffled.

Jarom stared pointedly at my nightstand and the ever-growing collection of pop cans, wrappers, and pizza crusts.

"To be fair, half of those are probably from the kids," I said sheepishly. Throwing myself down onto the pillow, I exclaimed, "Ugh! What is wrong with me? I was doing really well this summer. But now . . ." I blew a raspberry and gave the thumbs-down sign.

Jarom lay down beside me. "I know what you mean. It's been a year and a half, and we still don't have closet doors or baseboards," he said, referring to our recent house remodel.

"Guess we're both great at starting . . . not so good at finishing."

"True."

My husband listened patiently while I bemoaned my fat rolls for at least another half hour. I was too focused on my startling weight gain to let the truth of what I had just said sink in. A fire burned in my belly as I started thinking about the quickest way to drop fifty pounds. Upset made way for excitement. I was going to shed all these unwanted pounds . . . again. So what if I had done this same dance twenty times before? I was lost to the "starter's high." Like falling in love, starting a new project flooded my body with endorphins and gave me a single-minded focus on the task ahead, for at least a few weeks.

***

This was the simple truth that I had missed at the time. I was addicted to starting, but once that initial high faded and things got hard or boring, I would quit and start something else to get my next fix. I really should have seen it ages ago. My house is a monument to all the numerous things I've started over the years. You can't go five feet without running smack-dab into one of my grand plans.

Let's start in the garage. Buried deep in the back left corner, you would find everything you needed to start a small picture framing business. Sticks of molding, suede mats, glass, sample corners, and joining equipment sat unused, gathering dust. About four years before, we had a James Christensen print framed, and it cost about five hundred bucks.

Holy cow, the frame cost more than the print! With a little digging, we discovered that there was about a 400 percent markup on materials. Why spend a fortune when you could do it yourself? Better yet, why not make some money on the side framing things for friends and family. And so our little in-home business, Fit To Be Framed, was born. And here in the garage it was buried when we started the great house remodel. We tell ourselves that someday we'll dig all that stuff out again, when we have more time.

If you move on to the kitchen, you'll find a hodgepodge of kitchen cabinets. This was one of Jarom's projects. When we were remodeling the house, Jarom decided that he really wanted to make all the cabinets himself. So he bought a book, table saw, and planer, and started figuring out how to make cabinets. Since I really wanted a kitchen in the meantime, we collected old cabinets from family and filled in the holes with IKEA ones. Seamed together like Frankenstein, it was bulky, but it worked. Dreaming of the beautiful mission-style cabinets he would make, I waited. Life interfered, as it usually did, with work, kids, and a general lack of funds. Every time we pass through the kitchen, we remark on what a great kitchen we'll have . . . someday.

My craft room was a shrine to all the things I wanted to do. When I started having kids, I wanted to be the perfect mommy and cutely chronicle their every moment in a scrapbook. If the road to hell is paved with good intentions, then the path of good intentions is lined with scrapbook paper. The west wall had an eight-foot-tall by six-foot-wide shelving unit to organize and hold all the patterned paper I owned. There were bins for rubber stamps and bins for ink. Stacks of scrapbooks, some empty, some half filled, toppled over on the floor. Sacks of fabric sat abandoned next to the sewing machine and half-sewn quilt. Inside the desk were tools for stained glass and pane upon pane of glass in every color.

I loved to create (still do). Whenever I saw something cool that someone had made at the craft store or on TV, I had to run out, buy the materials, and try to make it. Inevitably, my creation looked nothing like the example, so I'd get disheartened and discouraged from any further attempts. So my collection grew and then sat, only to be dragged out to make the occasional thank-you card or for the annual church craft night. It was a tragedy to think of all things I could make but didn't. My husband claimed the real tragedy was all the money I'd spent on them.

There are so many more examples I could give, but the one that ate at my soul every time I passed it was the fourteen-year-old Kurzweil digital piano in the dining room. Oh, the plans I'd had for this one. In 1997, I was off to college to study music and become a world-renowned composer. Scrimping and saving all the money I could from a crappy telemarketing job, I went shopping for the piano that would help me fulfill my destiny. Tiny BYU housing meant that a baby grand was out of the question, so I went looking for an upright that took less space.

That's when I saw her— lacquered cherry wood and digital technology blended seamlessly into the most beautiful instrument I had ever seen. It had a floppy drive so you could record directly and transfer songs easily. There was a MIDI port that let you plug directly into a computer and print sheet music from your compositions. Harps, trumpets, violins—you could sound like a whole orchestra with this baby. This was my ticket; and for the small sum of six thousand dollars, this piano and I would conquer the world. Included in the purchase price was a two-hour recording session at the store. I couldn't have asked for anything more. Visions of cutting an album and becoming a superstar danced through my head.

In the beginning, I played every chance I could, some days racking up as much as six hours of practice time. Every spare moment not in class was spent with my new best friend. As for my dating life . . . well, who needed romance when you could write your own love song and record it for the world to hear?

But the world never heard it, because once the excitement of the dream wore off, the barbs of criticism and rejection rubbed me raw. Giving up, my dreams were locked away, and the piano went into storage until I got married and had a house of my own. Songs from the past were still stored on the hard drive; the piano's memory much better than my own. Sometimes I would hear their echoes, stirring feelings lying dormant, building until I was dizzy with the prospect of starting over and finally achieving my dreams. For more than ten years the cycle repeated itself, but like any addiction, the high I got from beginning again got shorter and less intense until one day the music stopped inspiring me at all. Now it sat silent in the foyer, a constant reminder of what I could've been and what I let slip away.

***

Diets had become much like the music. I had tried and failed so many times that it was nearly impossible to maintain the burning fever of purpose for more than a week. Sure, initially I would get pumped with the prospect of losing weight, but the idea of starving myself, taking pills, or whatever crazy thing I would try this time, got less appealing by the minute. However, there was one thing though that I always looked forward to when starting a new diet: "The Farewell Tour of Fast Food."

Each time I recommitted myself to eating healthier, I spent a few days saying good-bye to my dearest friends: Wendy, Ronald McDonald, the Colonel, Ben and Jerry, to name a few. Aside from the unfortunate side effect of an expanding waistline, these loyal companions had never let me down over the years. When I'd had a rough day at school, McD's had a meal guaranteed to make me "happy." C on a test? Wendy's french fries dipped in a Frosty helped with the disappointment. A+ on a test? Well, a milkshake or root beer float with my fried chicken would be perfect to celebrate. There was no heartache that a pint of Ben and Jerry's Cookie Dough couldn't soothe. When nobody else was around to listen to me cry at eleven o'clock at night, the fridge was always open and the drive-thru lane was "great even late." No matter the emotion, there was a snack for that. Comforting and constant, I could always count on my friends to help me weather the ups and downs of life and pant sizes. It would have been extremely rude to just quit visiting without some kind of closure.

I'm sure the tour added on a little weight, but what was one last pound or two when you already had to lose at least fifty? Planning my meal schedule carefully, I made sure to give my farewells to all my favorite foods. Who knew when I would have a chance to eat their calorie-rich goodness again? At each location, memories of past defeats and victories flavored every bite. Looking back now, I wonder if the real goal was to taste the yummy food or to ease the pain one more time. I don't honestly know. Food was a physical fix to an emotional problem. And if my waistline was any indication, then I had a lot of emotional problems to fix.

***

One of the reasons I selected the HCG diet this last time was because of the two "load" days. This diet actually had my farewell tour built in. The creator must have been fat himself and thus understood the need for closure. The diet protocol claimed you needed those first two days of fat loading to last you through the next three weeks of starvation. Whatever, I didn't care about the whys. All I cared about was what foods I could fit into those golden forty-eight hours. I made a list . . . a very long list. Didn't want to leave anything out.

For those two days, I ate anything and everything I could think of.

Cinnamon sweet rolls as soon as I woke up, then Krispy Kreme Donuts for brunch. For lunch, I decided on In-N-Out's double cheeseburger and fries. Halloween candy rapidly disappeared from the pumpkin-shaped bowl. Jarom even made my favorites for dinner, lasagna and spoon bread. Fortune smiled upon me because Ben and Jerry's had just released a limited batch of Pumpkin Cheesecake, a perfect midnight snack. Best day *ever*!

Until I woke up at about 4:00 a.m., sure I was going to die. Was it possible to overeat to the point of your stomach exploding? Because that's what it felt like. If I went to the hospital, I was sure the nurse would laugh at me and my stupidity, then send me home with a couple of Tums. So I just lay in bed and suffered in silence. In the morning, when it was time to do it all over again, I wanted to run and hide. Half of my list still remained, but the thought of putting a single thing in my mouth made me want to hurl.

I reread the HCG book to check if this reaction was normal, if I could skip the second load day, or if it had any references to possible tummy explosions. The only thing I could glean from my studies was the warning that if the load was not done correctly or skipped, then your diet would not be successful and no weight would be lost in the upcoming weeks. Well, there was no way that I was going to risk that, so I force fed myself the rest of my list. I choked down the French toast with caramel sauce and a side of Alka-Seltzer.

The rest of the day was a miserable disgusting blur that I've tried to block out. My stomach had never felt worse, and since I'd had a C-section with my second daughter, that was saying something. Later I went back and figured out that I had ingested approximately twelve thousand calories that weekend. When I weighed myself the following day I was a whopping five pounds heavier than the morning I heard the thud.

I'll give Dr. Simmeons, the HCG author, credit. If those two load days were an elaborate trick of reverse psychology, they totally worked. Never again would I binge on junk food when I was upset. I can't even look at a pint of Ben and Jerry's without the taste of bile at the back of my throat. What on earth was I doing to myself? Why did I keep putting my body through this crap? There's no way that this could be good for you. If you had asked me at the time my answer would have been that I was tired. Tired of being fat, so drastic measures were required because I couldn't bear the weight for one more day. If you asked me today, I would tell you it's because I was unhappy. Yes, unhappy with the way I looked, but I think the heaviness I felt was the weight of all the things I'd started but failed to finish hanging around my neck.

2

GHOSTS *of* FAT PAST

Around a month and a half later, I was down thirty-five pounds to 180/185, the same weight I was when I got married. You'd think I'd be happy when somebody gave me a compliment of how I looked. Instead I would smile and say thank you, but inside I was secretly thinking two things. First, that I was starving on five hundred calories a day, so I better look good. And second, I wondered what they were going to think if the weight came back on. Would they be surprised? Or would they say it was inevitable? Perhaps they'd even be disgusted. People close to me had been on this roller coaster before, so I envisioned them counting the weeks before the weight would begin creeping back on. Fear of gaining all I had lost plus a few extra kept me from enjoying the success of losing a size or two.

Christmas was two weeks away, and like Ebenezer Scrooge, I was haunted by ghosts of the past. The clock would strike one, but instead of the Ghost of Christmas Past, I would have the Ghosts of Fat Past, dozens lined up along the wall and out into the hallway. Each specter was a younger version of myself and an earlier diet attempt.

First in line was a chubby twelve-year-old girl. Just seeing her transformed my room into the vet's office where I first learned I was fat. My well-meaning but misguided father had me step on the scale that only moments before had been used to weigh our black Lab. One hundred twenty. So? Dad had to spell out it for me: B-I-G. My three sisters were all short and petite, but it looked like I was going to take after my plus-sized daddy. At almost five feet tall and 120 pounds, I was built more like a football player than a ballerina.

Heart-to-hearts were not my dad's strong suit. Poor guy. He had just gotten over the trauma of taking me to buy my first bra, and now he had to tell me I was fat. After the office visit, dad sat me down over a Diet Coke and awkwardly tried to warn me about my weight without causing me a lifetime of therapy. His life had been hell as the chubbiest kid at school. It didn't get any better the older and bigger he got.

One of the reasons he was confronting me now was that he had just lost 115 pounds, going from 285 pounds to 170. His doctor had prescribed the now defunct fen-phen (legal speed, basically) and a high-protein diet (precursor to the Atkins diet). Now he was like a new convert at church, wanting everyone else to join him in his enlightenment. Twice a week he would take me to the YMCA with him, so I could slim down by using the Stairmaster. (Seriously, what idiot came up with the stairway to nowhere?)

Satisfied with his missionary work, he gave me a bear hug, told me he loved me and asked if I understood that he only wanted the best for me. I remember nodding sagely and saying that I did, but all my twelve-year-old brain understood was that there was something wrong with me. It was like the old song from Sesame Street: "One of these things is not like the others. One of these things just doesn't belong." I was the odd man out in the family. Both mom and dad had slimmed down, and my sisters were naturally thin, so I was the only chunk. From that moment, I would scan the crowds for other little girls and critically assess if I was bigger than them. And if I was, then I would tell myself that I needed to work harder so I could look the same.

The next few teenage ghosts were proof that I never quite got there. I really came to treasure the days I spent with dad at the gym. But when he stopped going, his weight went up, and so did mine. Each year the scale added another ten pounds. I was always trying to find ways to get small. Since I was a complete klutz, school sports were out of the question, so I kept my attempts focused on what I ate. Or sometimes didn't eat. When I was unhappy about my looks, I would commit to starve myself until I looked better, thinner. Yeah, that lasted until dinner. Seeing an after-school special about bulimia on TV, I thought I'd give it a try. After the first dry heave, I resolved to never to do that on purpose again. My parents' doctor gave me some "vitamins" to boost energy and curb cravings, about eight pills a day. Total bust, but I want to go on the record that giving a teenager, especially a depressed teenager, a bunch of pills is a horrible idea. However, that's a whole different chapter.

My favorite ghost transported me back to my first year of college. I got hit with the freshmen fifteen . . . erm . . . twenty. The Atkins diet was the new hip story gracing all the women's magazine covers. Mom and I, both unpleasantly plump, decided to give it a whirl. It was initially a success. I lost twenty-eight pounds, which put me at about the same weight I was in eighth grade. But the distribution of those pounds was much better now that I was taller and had boobs.

My older but littler sister would flaunt her bag of Oreos at me, complaining snidely that she just couldn't gain weight no matter what she did. Those cookies looked good, but not as good as I did. All my hard work was paying off, and for the first time I was happy with my body. I finally had some self-confidence, and that was the first thing my husband-to-be noticed about me.

Jarom and I first met on a big group date to see the Christmas lights in Salt Lake City. The power I had gained from my very first diet success was a heady thing. Feeling bold and unstoppable, I tried my hand at flirting. Since I was an amateur, it was more along the lines of grade school flirting, where I teased him about his awful cowboy boots and called him Cowboy. He reciprocated and teased me for being so perky, calling me Sunshine. We were both so bad at the whole courtship ritual, we really were the perfect match. After we had both gone home, he told one of our mutual friends that I was completely psychotic, but that didn't stop him from asking me out for New Year's Eve, and every week after.

Having my first real boyfriend was great for my social calendar, but not so good for diet plans. It started out small with one pound here and there from our dates to Olive Garden. Then came the break-ups and the make-ups. Being an emotional eater, it was easy to find an excuse to indulge in chocolaty therapy. By the time we got married a year and a half later, I had put back on the twenty-eight pounds I had lost and gained another ten to boot. Doesn't exactly make for the ideal bridal gown fitting does it?

The remaining spirits represented the next ten and a half years that I waged war on the fat. Short of surgical solutions, I had tried every fad, celebrity-recommended diet out there. Cleanse diets, packaged meal plans, ephedrine products. I even tried ordering myself a Bowflex Body. Who knew you actually had to work to get that body and not just pay the six installments of $99.99? When popular diets failed, I thought up my own. Once my brother in-law hosted a weight-loss competition, so I came up with the Five-Bite Diet, (patent pending). Basically you could eat whatever you wanted in a meal, but only five bites. Portion control at its finest, but it worked. I won the contest, took home the fifty bucks, and enjoyed being a size ten for about two months. Then like every other plan mentioned, as soon as the diet stopped, the weight crawled or jumped back on.

Constant practice had made me a pro at losing weight; I even lost weight when I was pregnant. It was effortless in the sense that I didn't try, but let me tell you that throwing up every single day for nine months was not easy. Both times after the girls were born, I was thirty pounds less than when I started. You'd think that with a big head start like that and a year of nursing ahead, I would have continued to whittle away the fat. Wrong. As soon as throwing up ended and I was able to eat again, the pounds flew onto my butt and tummy. I told myself that I needed the extra six cinnamon rolls since I was nursing and thereby eating for two. Blame the nine months of forced bulimia, but my appetite was unending. After a year of nursing my last daughter, Autumn, I was bigger than ever before topping the scale at the thud-worthy 216.6 I told you about.

**

Rehashing every bad dieting experience was exhausting. But now the ghosts were gone and, Dickens be darned, I could finally sleep. In reality, sleep rarely came anymore, and my mind constantly raced with worries and worst-case scenarios. What was I going to do now? How was I going to keep the fat away for good? Tomorrow, the HCG diet would be officially over and I could finally start eating more than three slices of turkey breast and an apple two times a day. Aside from the whole starving part, it had been easy since I'd been told exactly what and how much to eat. But now I was going to be on my own, the book saying only to slowly add foods back into your diet. Where was the chapter with detailed meal plans, and just how slow was "slowly"?

Panicked, I leapt from the bed and hopped onto the Internet. Surely there must be forum for this. Every site I clicked had horror stories of what happened in the maintenance phase. Some people now found themselves allergic to dairy for first time, or worse, intolerant to wheat. What if that happened to me? I've already established that the whole no-bread thing wouldn't work for me. Page after page, I found instances of dieters gaining weight but saying that it was okay because they could just do the HCG diet again.

Oh heck no. There was no way that I could ever do another three weeks of five hundred calories a day. My nose started to tickle and my vision blurred. I heard a voice.

It's hopeless. Within six months you'll be even fatter than before.

Was someone there? Jarom was snoring loudly, so unless he had recently learned ventriloquism, it wasn't him.

You can't do it. As soon as you go back to eating all that crap you normally do, you'll be a failure . . . again.

Wait, I knew this voice. It was the little voice in my head that reminded me of all the things I'd screwed up. No, I'm not schizophrenic; I didn't hear actual voices; they were just my own thoughts replaying all my failures on an endless loop with bonus snide commentary. Dickens's ghosts would have been a welcome exchange—at least they came once and left Scrooge alone. But my ghost stayed with me as my constant companion. Though I referred to it as a ghost, perhaps demon would be more accurate. Surely, a voice that said so many evil discouraging things must be from hell. Whatever it was, it had held power and sway over me and my decisions for years.

Born from failures and self-loathing, it rose from the darkest parts of my soul. Whenever the high and initial excitement of starting a new project faded, that little voice was there, waiting in the background for its opportunity to strike. In my hometown in West Virginia, I had been a big fish in a little pond. At thirteen years old, I composed a five-movement piece for piano, then moved on to writing ensemble pieces. At sixteen, I left high school to go to college so I could become a famous composer. I bought my precious piano, ready to blow everyone away.

When I got there, no one was terribly impressed with what I'd done, and I learned that I was now a very little fish in a very big ocean. Every time I heard someone criticize my work, my mind would burn it into memory for future playback. Soon, for every compliment I received, my mind would repeat five earlier complaints. Performing became next to impossible for me because I was listening to the little voice instead of the music. I never even officially declared my major because I was so terrified that I wasn't good enough to pass the initial entrance auditions.

Everyone else is so much better than you. How could you miss that chord?

Geez, do you need a metronome? A five-year-old could have played that better than you. You really need to practice more. Ha, and you thought you were something special. You so don't belong here.

And after telling myself that long enough, I decided it must be true. I didn't belong with that caliber of musicians, so I quit school and quit music all together. And that's why the piano just sits in my home, because I hadn't been able to find joy in the music again, not while reminding myself that I hadn't been able to hack it, that I'd quit.

Same thing happened with my next pursuit, writing. When music didn't pan out, I went with my second love of storytelling. I'm a bookworm, and when life isn't too hectic, I can read a book a day. From sci-fi and grocery store romances to literary classics and nonfiction, I loved the written word. Every once and a while the book I'd chosen would be terrible and I would think, "Hey, I can write better than this, so if this junk can be published, then so can I."

Poised at the computer, I would begin to pen the next great novel. The words flowed through my brain and out through my fingers, the rhythmic keystrokes creating their own kind of music. Before I knew it, I had fifty pages finished and ready for edits. The first read-through I would be really excited, only changing small grammatical errors, adding commas, and so on. I would pump myself up thinking about my name on the *New York Times* bestseller list, maybe even getting interviewed on the *Today Show*. Second and third read-throughs were met with less enthusiasm, and I started hacking out sentences and big chunks of paragraphs. With each edit, I doubted more and more my ability to be an author. The little voice would pop up and agree.

Are you that arrogant to think that people would pay to read something you wrote. Come on. This is the dumbest story I have ever heard. You'll never finish it, and even if you did, no agent would take it, let alone a publishing house. Maybe you can wallpaper your office with the rejection letters. This sentence right there is so trite, like a junior high book report. Wouldn't it be better to give up now while you can still pretend you have talent? They can't tell you it sucks if no one ever reads it.

Once again, I berated myself into quitting because I was afraid that everything I was telling myself was true. Experience and that voice were my most trusted teachers, showing me that I was nobody and nothing. Better yet, if you didn't put yourself out there, you couldn't get stepped on. So that's what I did—I stopped trying altogether.

I literally lived in bed during some periods of my life because I was afraid of everything and had regular panic attacks from the thought of talking to any human being. They would laugh at me, judge me, and see through me. I was convinced that if I couldn't love me, then everyone else must despise me. Funny thing about hiding though: no matter how deeply I was buried under the covers, I couldn't escape myself.

My mind told me the world was full of monsters ready to tear me apart, but in truth, the only monster was in my head. Looking back, it's sad and ironic. I turned away friends and opportunities because I was afraid they would hurt and reject me. The problem was that even the harshest of criticisms from someone else wouldn't come close to the things I said to myself.

I even went so far as to turn from God for a time. When you took away school, hobbies and friends, then the only thing left I had left to destroy was my faith. And make no mistake, that's exactly what that little voice was doing, destroying everything good in my life. Already on shaky ground, it didn't take much convincing to think that even heaven wouldn't take me.

Focusing on the list of things that a good Christian woman should be, I found my own list bleak and lacking. My home was always dirty, my husband and I didn't have family prayer or scripture study, and I quit sewing after I sewed through my thumb. I almost burned down the house the last time I tried to make baked potatoes, so making bread from scratch was completely out of the question.

In my eyes, the sins were endless. From occasionally swearing to the time I gossiped and hurt a little girl's feelings back in sixth grade, repenting never touched the memories etched in stone. Religion should have been a comfort for me, a shield against the world that scared me. Instead it became the courtroom where all my failures were laid bare.

Someone so flawed and broken could never make it into the Lord's presence.

The pain that one little thought caused surpassed any that I had ever felt. Even God wouldn't want me. So I went on the offense, telling myself he didn't exist, because, after all, you couldn't be judged by a God if there wasn't one, right?

***

But that didn't solve the problem. The little voice continued to belittle me every chance it had, chipping away any self-worth that I gained when I lost weight, building walls that kept me from finishing anything and reaching my goals. So when, in the middle of the night, it resurfaced again, reminding me that my success wouldn't last, I crawled back in bed next to my husband and wept. My poor dear husband just couldn't catch a good night's sleep because even though I tried to be silent, I am not a quiet crier. Leaking tears turned to loud racking sobs that would have woken the dead.

Jarom rolled over and opened one eye partway. "Wassup? Somun rung?"

I don't remember what I said or how much of it he could understand being half asleep, but it was to the effect that I was scared that when I started eating normally I would get fat and that I was tired and couldn't live with myself if I failed again.

"Hmphm. You're fine. You'll think of something . . ."

The next minute I remember exactly. "The only thing I can think of is that I'm going to do something wrong."

"Then tell your thinker to shut up and do something about it. Now go to sleep."

How rude! Just like that he dropped back off and started sawing logs again. Did he really just tell me to shut up? The stupidhead. That's it—I was filing for divorce in the morning. I went to bed in a huff, my mind too busy worrying about the cost of the attorney to think about voices or Dickens's ghosts. When confronted in the morning, my husband claimed innocence and had no recollection of our conversation. How convenient for him. Well, I did, and I would remind him. So I told him what he said, word for word.

"Huh. Seems like pretty sound advice to me." He patted himself on the back for being so smart, even if he didn't remember it. "Stop worrying about it and do something. Don't even try to think about it anymore. Nothing good could come out of it, so just turn your brain off. "

Now it was my turn to go "Huh." I guess it couldn't hurt to try. Don't think about it, don't worry about it—just do whatever I had to do to keep going. For a stupidhead, I guess my husband was pretty smart after all.

3

WELCOME *to* *the* FAT PACK

When I was a kid, my grandma was obsessed with Richard Simmons. So when she visited for a week, we would sweat to the oldies, and when she left, I'd go back to being a lump.

As an adult, quick weight loss and fad diets had never managed to keep the weight off, so I decided once the diet was over I was going to have to take a proactive approach to weight management. The problem with being proactive lies in the root word: active. I've had a passing acquaintance with exercise in the past but never formed a meaningful relationship.

I had gone to the gym for six months with my dad. In high school my mom enrolled me in cheerleading classes, but after two lessons, the instructor said it was hopeless and gave her back her money. Then nothing until I met my husband who was an avid hiker, rock climber, and mountaineer. If I wanted to keep his interest, I had to fool him into thinking I was into all those things too. So I feigned enthusiasm because I loved him way more than I hated hiking. I bought hundreds of dollars in rock climbing gear so I could go with him and try to reach the top, sure that if I did, he'd be mine. I sucked at it, but he must've appreciated the effort because he married me anyway.

I'm ashamed to say that as soon as the ink on the marriage license was dry, I magically lost all interest in the outdoors. Jarom would take me camping and try to coax me up a mountain. I'd make it maybe a quarter of the way and stop, my motivation to prove myself gone since he'd already put a ring on it. Armed with a good book, I would urge him on and plop myself down and await his return. Three or four hours later, he'd find me where he left me and we would traverse the steep descent. He would bound down the slick rock like a mountain goat. I would slide down most of the way on my bum, more often than not ripping a giant hole in the seam of my pants. Half of the pictures from those trips and climbs feature what I call the baboon butt: a shot of me from behind, pants ripped open showing a big patch of whatever color underwear I was wearing.

Yep, exercise and I were not friends. But no matter how many times I had told this to my doctor, he insisted that I needed it to be healthy. For years I'd scoffed that being healthy was overrated, but now I wasn't so sure. Before the thud, I would go to the doctor with complaints of lethargy, depression, and feeling generally like roadkill. He ran tests but warned that he already knew what the results would be. I was obese, maybe even morbidly obese, and prediabetic to boot. Unless I started exercising and losing weight, I was going to keep being miserable until I died.

That sounded a little harsh to me. I was fat, but morbidly obese? Puh-lease. I just had a slow metabolism, that's all. Maybe I could take some thyroid pills or something—that would speed it up. Doctor said nope: the only way I was going to feel better was to start exercising because even though it defied logic, apparently the moving around gave you more energy. It's totally a case of the chicken and the egg. If I had more energy, then maybe I'd move more, but I couldn't get more energy until I moved. The circular logic gave me a headache.

Now that my thinker was supposed to be turned off, I needed to go out there and just do. But do what? Jarom suggested hiking again. Um, no. It was winter, and slogging through snow might be great for burning calories, but it sounded like my version of hell literally being frozen over. Biking? Nope, I was not going to get squished by a car that skidded on black ice. Out of ideas, Jarom remembered that earlier that year I had joined a gym in a moment of insanity.

"Hey, do you still belong to that gym down the road?"

I cringed. I'd meant to cancel the membership, but the $29.99 was still being deducted every month from my checking account. For once my propensity for procrastination was going to pay off. I wasn't going to have to go gym shopping; it was traumatic enough the first time.

***

Finding a gym is a lot like buying a used car; it's a big commitment and involves pushy obnoxious salespeople who want you to spend way more than you need to. When I started looking around, trying to find the best gym, one of the most important factors for me was the length of contract. I was completely amazed to find out that some of these gyms wanted you to sign a two-year contract of around forty dollars a month. Oh, and by the way, if they close that particular location, as long as there was another in the chain within twenty miles, you were still obligated to pay.

Seriously? Not only did they want me to commit to the idea that I will be working out for the next two years (which considering I couldn't commit to a hair color for that long seemed unlikely), but if they close the gym that I visit, they still expected me to pay for the privilege of driving twenty minutes each way to get sweaty and stinky. No, thank you.

That old dusty Bowflex was starting to look better, but still I persevered until I found a "fitness club" about a mile from my house that billed month to month. It sounded too good to be true. I could quit when I wanted to and not be stuck on the hook for another twenty-three months? Sign me up.

If only it were that easy. Before you sign the paper, they have to tell you all about their personal training service, and lucky you, they're running a special so you get a free session. Now you're stuck at peak business hours in a Lycra tank top and shorts that show every roll and bump in the wall-to-wall mirrors, with some kid, who can't be more than twelve, attempting to show you the proper push-up position.

And then at the end of your "free" session, you get a ten-minute high-pressured sales pitch to enroll in the sixty-five-dollars-an-hour personal training program. Amazingly after the first no, they're having a special with three sessions for a hundred dollars. Before you have a chance to say no again, they subtly remind you why you're there . . . because you're fat.

"You want to see results, don't you? And so far, going it alone hasn't really worked out for you, has it?"

I admit it: I was weak. One week later, I was one pound and a hundred bucks lighter. I had at least fifty pounds to lose . . . do the math. Personal training was not the right fit for me or my wallet. I much preferred humiliating myself without an audience, even one I'd paid for.

In the middle of the day, the gym was infested with gym rats and gym bunnies. Gym rats are the guys that work out in small groups. Big and beefy, they stare at themselves in the mirror and flex their muscles while they take turns spotting each other on the bench press. They aren't so bad because they're too busy admiring their own reflections to notice anyone else. Much worse are the gym bunnies with their perfectly coiffed hair and makeup, looking more like they're about to enter a beauty pageant than exercise. They'll jog slowly or walk on the treadmill, glancing critically around the room, checking out the competition. Phone in hand, they text constantly and laugh conspiratorially at some inside joke.

It's like high school all over again. Well, I was too old for high school, so I ditched the midday workouts and started stalking the gym, driving by at all hours looking for an empty parking lot—10:00 p.m. was the sweet spot.

Thirty minutes on the elliptical machine was the most I could do at first. Even that much was exhausting and a real effort to complete. I won't lie, some days I walked in and after five minutes walked back out. The voice in my head would tell me how ridiculous I looked and remind me of how nice and cozy my bed would feel. So I'd give up, go home, and go to sleep. Eventually I skipped the whole going part and talked myself out of it before I left the house.

***

Starting again this time, my thinker was supposed to be off, and thirty minutes was a long time, so I would need a distraction. I tried to read, but I bounced too much and just got seasick. Next I bought an audiobook on iTunes and swore that I'd only listen to it while I was at the gym. Unfortunately I picked a really good book, so unable to put it away, I kept my headphones on long after I was home. It's a lot easier to follow the story line when your heavy breathing doesn't drown out the narrator.

Finally I settled on making a playlist for my iPod. The songs I chose were catchy and fast-paced, easy to move to. I made little inside jokes with my choices like "Shut Up and Let Me Go" by the Ting Tings or "Misery Business" by Paramore, timed to play just when my legs were hurting and I wanted to go home. And when my little voice popped up, trying to persuade me that leaving ten minutes early wouldn't hurt anything, I made sure I couldn't think anymore. After all, you can't think and sing at the same time.

If no one else was there, I belted it out with conviction, and if I had company I sung softly with gusto. I enjoyed it. It was fun. Sure I got some odd looks, but either no one had the courage to talk to the deranged lady on the elliptical, or they just turned their music up louder. Every day that I kept doing my thing, it got easier, and I started staying longer. The thirty minutes turning into thirty-five . . . forty . . . until I was starring in my own sixty-minute version of *American Idol*—cardio edition.

Six nights a week I would put in my hour at the gym, then come home and practically pass out from sheer exhaustion. For the first time in years I was actually sleeping through the night, since even my mind was too wiped out to race. During the day I had more energy, probably because I was finally getting some sleep.

Even though my focus had been on maintaining the weight I'd lost, the pounds kept slipping off, and I wasn't going to complain. Let them keep coming if they wanted to. When I looked in the mirror, I saw a smaller me. My little voice would pipe in and say "still flabby though." Continuing the theme from earlier, I would say to myself "shut up" and then go do something about it.

I remembered from my failed personal training sessions that if I wanted to tone up, I would need to do some strength training. Weight machines and equipment scared me. I had visions of being alone in the gym and getting trapped under a massive barbell. No one would find my crushed corpse until the next morning and my cause of death would be "squished by good intentions." It was probably a good idea to go when a few other people were around so that someone could help me when I'd inevitably scream, "I've fallen and I can't get up."

As soon as the kids were tucked in bed, I headed out to the gym. If I had taken a minute to read the schedule, I would have seen that there was a fitness class being held at that time, Cardio Body Blast. The first few times I watched surreptitiously out the corner of my eye. I remember thinking, "These ladies are nuts!" Music was blaring, the trainer was yelling like a drill sergeant, and four slightly squishy women were doing squats . . . on the treadmill . . . while it was moving. Where on earth did someone come up with that horrible idea? I hoped the gym was current on its insurance premiums because if those ladies were anything like me, then someone was about to go flying.

After the song ended, they hopped off the machines and gave each other high fives and hugs. Though they had just finished what looked like a completely brutal workout, their faces brimmed with pride as they congratulated each other. My sidelong glances must have turned into full-blown gawking because a face popped up next to my weights.

"You're welcome to join us, you know. We have fun, it's free, and it's easier to keep going when other people are pushing you to do your best."

From anyone else that line would have sounded like another sales pitch, but this tiny little woman radiated sincerity. She was cute and perky and had huge dimples and twinkly eyes that crinkled slightly at the corners, normally the kind of girl I would hate on sight. She kept prattling on about all the benefits of group exercise, and maybe it was her infectious grin or lack of guile, but instead of feeling intimidated or jealous of her size-two body, I found myself actually liking her. I agreed noncommittally to give it a shot one of these days. Next Tuesday found me five minutes early, nervously waiting for class to start.

What if I was horrible at . . . whatever this was? What if I looked stupid, and did they really need floor-to-ceiling mirrors everywhere? Maybe it was a plus for gym rats and gym bunnies, but I for one did not enjoy watching my fat jiggle when I did jumping jacks. I almost turned around and left the gym, claiming I left the fridge open or the stove on. Kelly Clarkson's "My Life Would Suck Without You" blared out of the sound system, and I was trapped. I was going to have to see this through. The trainer bounced up to the front of the room, welcomed me, and introduced herself as Sarah Michelle. Around the room, everyone else did the same—Susan, Sharon, Mallory.

Apparently I had picked the wrong day to start this, because today was the day of the month they did an Insanity theme, based on the popular workout program. Every thirty seconds, the trainer called out a different exercise and you just kept going nonstop for thirty minutes. The theory behind it being "You can do anything for only thirty seconds." Ha! They hadn't met me yet.

The pace was so frenzied that I didn't have a chance to worry how foolish I looked. Those thirty seconds of sit-ups were the longest of my entire life. Sarah claimed that they were supposed to work your ab core; I was pretty sure I didn't have one of those. Insanity was aptly named, because you would have to be crazy to do this regularly.

The buzzer went off, signaling the end of the thirty minutes. Saved by the bell, literally, because I am pretty sure that even five more seconds of push-ups would have killed me. Lying half dead on the mat, I was filled with pride. I had survived, it wasn't pretty and I'm sure that a proper push-up meant your tummy was supposed to leave the ground, but I had stayed the whole time. I rolled over and attempted to right myself when Sarah shouted to grab some weights: it was pump time.

I'm not ashamed to say that I cried a little bit. Thankfully, you couldn't separate the tears from the sweat. Though the thirty-minute Insanity portion was over, there was still thirty minutes left of free weights. Taking the longest walk to the water fountain in history, I mentally prepared myself to keep going. I'd felt so good when I thought I'd lasted the whole class, and I wanted to feel that again instead of the disappointment I associated with quitting.

Looking around the room, I could see the other women already had their weights and were waiting for me to get mine. Their little black weights all said eight pounds on them. That sounded like an awful lot, but I didn't want to look like a weenie by grabbing a pair of five-pounders, so I grabbed the eights.

Big mistake. When Sarah had us lift the weights over our heads and bend them back for a tricep curl, my weights were too heavy for my underdeveloped sausage arms. Instead of bending my elbows back in a controlled descent, the weights swung behind me, right into the back of my head. In automatic reaction to the pain, I dropped my weights, hitting my heel. I looked like a human flamingo trying to balance on my left leg with one hand holding my head, the other hand holding up my bruised heel.

When the blood stopped thumping in my ears, I listened for the mocking peals of laughter. I waited, but they never came. A few sympathetic chuckles maybe. One of the girls, Mallory, threw an arm around me and swore she'd nearly done the same thing once. Three other heads nodded in agreement. When I looked them in the eye, I saw plenty of concern for my bleeding heel and growing goose egg, but none of the judgment I had come to fear and expect.

Sarah Michelle was shocked when I showed up to class the next week. She had been sure after last time's disaster that I would have been embarrassed or afraid to come back. I assured her that she couldn't get rid of me that easy. Not anymore, that is. Sure I'd spent the rest of the week nursing my head and limping down the stairs, but I also spent the week feeling great about finding new friends and a new sense of accomplishment. Not only had I accomplished nearly knocking myself out, but, wanting to show my new buddies I was tough, I still finished the class afterward. I may have hated the soreness I felt the next day when I discovered that I did indeed have abs, but I loved everything else that hour gave me.

***

Over the next six months, those ladies and I bonded with every grunt and groan. Sinatra had his Rat Pack, but I had these ladies, which I deemed my Fat Pack. Some of us had more inches to lose than others and did so with varying degrees of success, but there was a support and camaraderie that I grew to depend on. When Lori joined our group, she felt bad that she needed to start with three-pound weights. Recounting the tough time I had when I first started, we told her it was better to have little weights than a big headache. Just knowing someone had been there before, and did much worse, was enough to get her to come back next week and join the pack.

Somewhere along the way, I started looking forward to my time at the gym. It had become the release I needed after a stressful day. I was happier and healthier than I had ever been. My mother insisted that I should go back to the doctor since all this happiness and exercising just wasn't like me.

When the doctor saw me, he was surprised by my new look but, more important, my new outlook. He barely managed to keep the smug out of his voice when he said, "I told you so" about the benefits of exercise. I was feeling great! Not only did he give me a clean bill of health that I could show my mom, but since my mood had improved so much, he also took me off the antidepressants I had been on since I was fifteen. Not having to remember to take those horrible pills every morning was the icing on the cake (that I still wasn't allowed to eat).

4

RUNNING IS CHEAPER *than* THERAPY

One day, Jarom and I were walking the girls to the park when out of the blue he turned to me and said, "Let's run a marathon."

Running. Haha, that was funny. The only good reason to run was if someone was chasing you, and even then it was debatable.

"Excuse me? I don't think I heard that right. Because I thought I heard you say that we should run a marathon, but that would be crazy since neither one of us can outrun the four-year-old."

"I'm serious. You see, I bought this book . . ." He then began to extol the amazing qualities of said book.

Oh heavens, here we go. Everything Jarom knows in life, he learned from a book. When he decided to wire all the electrical in the house, he bought a book. When he decided he wanted to be a software engineer, he bought a programming manual. Our bookshelves were lined with books on gardening, water features, cabinet making, and even rooftop astronomy. What's worse is that it actually works for him! Whatever he reads, suddenly he can do it. It's incredibly annoying since anytime I try to read a textbook my head hurts and I get all cross-eyed from confusion. This time, he had apparently bought a book on marathon training.

Interrupting his oral book report, I asked him just one question. "Why?"

He looked down, and honest to goodness, started shuffling his feet like he was embarrassed. "Well, I've kinda always wanted to run one, but I was afraid to do it by myself. And before when you were . . . um . . . bigger, there was no chance that you'd ever do it with me. But now that you're losing weight and getting fit, it should be really easy for you. I'm sure you'll run laps around me."

Flattery will get you nowhere, buddy, but he did have a point. With forty-five pounds of fat off so far, running would be easier than before, and it might help me lose even more. After all, how many fat runners do you know? But this marathon business was out of the question. Did he even know how long a marathon was? Twenty-six point two mind-numbing miles. Perhaps he was confused and meant to say a 5K. A 5K run/walk seemed doable. I turned around to tell him so, but he must have seen rejection in my face because he preempted me with a guilt attack.

"You know, Dr. Slack told me that exercise would really help get my diabetes under control. But if you don't want to help me with that, I understand. You might have to be a single mother though, since I'll prob-ably die young." He sighed dramatically and pushed the stroller in front of me.

Really? When did Jarom learn to channel the spirit of my friend's Yiddish grandmother? She's the only other person I knew that used the threat of imminent death quite so effectively. But I supposed since he had been supportive of my weight loss, I could be supportive of his . . . midlife crisis or whatever this was.

And that's why I started running. To be honest, I figured since I was in a little better shape than him (after all, I'd been going to the gym now for two whole months, a new record) all I would have to do was keep run-ning until he quit first, and that would be the end of that. I had no clue that by agreeing to run with my husband, I was signing up for life lessons with a side of knee pain.

***

According to all the experts, when you started running, the first thing you had to do was buy a good pair of running shoes. That couldn't be too hard, right? Go to the store, get a cute size 7 that's cheap, and be done with it. When I got the running store, I found out how wrong I was.

First question the clerk asked me was if I was an underpronater or an overpronater. I didn't think that was any of his business. Then he guided me to the never-ending wall of shoes. Apparently there was more to picking a shoe than just color choices. Each pair of shoes had a different purpose—ones for stability, motion control, extra cushioning, racing flats, and those barefoot thingies that look like socks. He explained the grave consequences of choosing the wrong shoe: arch problems, IT band problems, plantar fasciitis, losing toenails, knee replacements.

It should be noted that I have a giant phobia of being wrong. It colors everything I do. I have trouble picking the restaurant because I'm afraid I'll pick the wrong one and no one else will like it, or someone will get food poisoning and then it will be my fault because I picked the restaurant. I had been okay with choosing my own shoes when I thought I only had to worry about matching my new running outfit. Now this guy was telling me that my choice had bigger consequences than just a fashion faux pas. That freaked me out! What if I made the wrong choice and crippled myself?

So as usual, I didn't make a choice at all. I walked out of the store and started to run in my well-loved, worn out hiking shoes. Turns out not making a decision was probably the worse decision I could make. Within a week, my left knee hurt if I even thought about running. I had blisters on my heels, between my toes, and I think a blister might have started forming under my toenail if that was possible. Who knew hiking shoes did not make good running shoes? Aside from you and probably 90 percent of the population, my husband did. That's why the next Saturday, Jarom packed the kids in the car and marched me back into the running store.

Of course the same clerk was there with a huge "I knew you'd be back" grin on his face. If he said I told you so, he could kiss his commission good-bye. Since I still had no idea what kind of shoe I needed, he had me try on a variety in the size sevens I requested. When I didn't like the feel of any of those, he wisely decided to measure my feet and then disappeared in the back room. My best friend, Misty, had been preaching the religion of shoe shopping for years, but personally I thought this was more like purgatory than heaven. I looked over at Jarom, who was too busy taking a sports bra off my daughter Lily's head to be of any help.

The clerk returned with a box that said Saucony. Since I have really bad eyesight, I read it as Saucy, so when he opened the box I expected the shoes inside to reflect that and be cute and "saucy," maybe even pink. Boy, was I wrong. They were ugly white sneakers with a blue slash on the side.

But that was not the most offensive thing. The biggest problem was that the tag said size 8 wide. Excuse me? Maybe I was being overly sensitive, but I was a little upset that this clerk thought that I had fat feet. When I pointed out that he had obviously grabbed the wrong size, he said nothing and laced them onto my feet.

So on my twelfth pair of shoes, I had a Cinderella moment. The skies opened up, angels sang a heavenly chorus, and I knew these ugly, expensive, most comfortable shoes on the planet would take me where I needed to go. I was in love.

I left that store two hundred dollars poorer, but I gained new insight. How many great things had I missed out on in life because I had been afraid of picking the wrong one? Never again would I let the fear of being wrong keep me from something I enjoyed. From then on when it was my turn to choose a place to eat, I was not going to defer to someone else and eat lukewarm Mexican. No, if I wanted sushi, then by golly we would have sushi and I would love it.

***

Next on the list of things Jarom's book said I needed to be a runner was a positive attitude. Haha, fat chance. It's pretty tough to have a positive attitude about something when you were counting down the days until you could quit. But never let it be said that I didn't give it a shot. Running a marathon is supposedly 10 percent physical and 90 percent mental, so I needed to develop a strong will to carry me through the tough spots. Unfortunately for me, my tough spots were so plentiful that they glommed together to make a seamless solid.

Not a single part of this running thing was easy. From squeezing into running tights, to figuring out the stupid heart rate watch, to huffing and puffing down the track, it all basically sucked. And that is exactly what I was thinking as I ran down the track. "This sucks . . . huff huff . . . this really sucks." So yeah, I probably didn't have that positive attitude they were talking about. The book provided mental exercises along with the physical ones to prepare you to run the marathon. It was glorified self-affirmations for the most part.

I'd had a therapist that tried to get me to do the same thing once. The way he explained it was that if you heard something often enough, you would believe it. Unfortunately for most of us, we hear all the negative things and start to believe that. (Yup, I had that part down pat.) So the whole point of self-talking was to change the dialogue, so you were hearing more positive things. I thought it was a little odd for a therapist to be encouraging you to talk to yourself, but sure, I could give it a try.

I felt like a total idiot. Seriously, what on earth are you supposed to say? "Um, hello, me . . . I guess you're not totally lame . . . your hair looks good today." This is why I had no imaginary friends as a kid. They all thought I was boring and found somebody else's imagination to play with.

I asked Jarom what he was planning to say to himself. Maybe I could swipe some ideas off him.

"Yeah, I'm skipping that part of the book."

"You can't skip part of the book. Is that even legal?"

Jarom snorted his reply.

Okay then. But I was curious what would make do-it-by-the-letter Jarom skip a set of instructions. "Well fine, then. At least tell me why."

"It reminds me too much of Stuart Smalley."

"Who's Stuart Smalley?"

"He was a character sketch on Saturday Night Live years ago. Remember, he would stand in front of the mirror and say 'I'm good enough, I'm smart enough, and, gosh darnit, people like me.'"

I'd forgotten the name from the show, but I totally remembered that guy. He was sad and pathetic and hilarious all at the same time. He always wore these horrible Cosby sweaters and had this really weird effeminate voice when he said his daily affirmations. I definitely agreed with Jarom on this one. I did not want to be that guy.

I decided that I too would skip that part of the book. That is, until my iPod died after three miles on a four-mile run. My first thought was "Eh, this is close enough. I don't really need to finish the whole four miles." Second thought was "Shut up and run." That worked for about five seconds, and then my feet got really heavy like I was slogging through mud.

I wanted to go home, but I only had a few laps of the park to go. I can lie to myself really well, but I can't fib to another person and keep a straight face. So I knew when I got home Jarom would ask if I did the whole four miles, and I would have to tell him the truth. I wanted that truth to be yes, so I needed to figure out a way to haul my butt around the loop one and a half more times.

For whatever reason, the face of Stuart Smalley appeared in my head. What the hey—couldn't hurt, right? I wasn't about to say his mantra, even in my head, so I had to come up with my own. I came up with "I can do it. I am awesome." I would repeat that over and over, timing the pounding of feet to the syllables until I got my rhythm back. It got easier and I was too tired to feel stupid.

But when it was time to climb the last little hill, my feet slowed down of their own accord. I fought to keep my feet in line with my words. I was struggling so hard against the weight of my legs that just before the crest of the hill, I yelled out my mantra at the top of my lungs. The cute little old lady from across the way was getting her mail and shouted back, "Sure you are, honey!" My face was already beet red from exertion, but if were possible, it got even redder. She might have thought I was a lunatic, but she waved politely anyway and went back inside. But crazy or not, it had worked and I crossed the four-mile marker. I started using variations of my chant to help me through the rough stretches, but I tried to restrain myself from any more blurting.

***

For my birthday, Jarom took me on a shopping spree. Most of my friends would have squealed with glee, but I had mixed emotions. On one hand, running and exercise had helped me shed twenty pounds more since the HCG diet (for those of you keeping score, that's a total of fifty-five pounds), so I desperately needed new clothes. On the other hand, what if I tried on the smaller clothes and they didn't fit me? What if I still had to shop in the big girl's section? Before the thud I had been a 16/18 XXL, and since I hadn't bought any new clothes in a while, I had no idea what size I was now. I realize it makes no sense, but I was afraid that I would still be unable to fit well in an extra large.

I remembered the lesson I had learned from my running shoes and decided not to let fear stop me from enjoying my birthday. It was the big 3-0 after all. We went up to the Factory Outlet Mall because I love a good deal. And that's why when we walked into the Columbia store, I made a beeline over to their 50-percent-off rack. I was dismayed when I found out that everything on the rod was from a sample sale, so all the sizes were mediums. It didn't even occur to me that these would be an option for me, so I walked back over to Jarom.

"Wasn't there anything over there that you liked?" he asked.

"Plenty, but they're all mediums."

"And what size are you?"

"I don't know, but not a medium."

"How do you know unless you try it on?"

I rolled my eyes. "Because I couldn't wear a medium when I was twelve years old, so I'm pretty sure it won't fit now."

"Humor me." Jarom grabbed a handful of hangers and thrust them into my arms.

"Whatever." I sulked off to the dressing room.

I stripped off my sweats and grabbed a random hanger. Green cargo pants that looked mighty small to me. If I ripped the stitching trying these on, then Jarom was paying for them and not out of my birthday money. I actually closed my eyes while I zipped them up, like that would help them fit better. Back to the mirror, I opened one eye and then the other and then looked down. No split seams that I could see. Better brave the mirror and check the backside.

I did not recognize the girl I saw standing there. Obviously, the logical side of my brain knew I had gotten smaller, but the emotional side hadn't figured it out till just then. I had been wearing sweats and drawstring pants that hid my progress from critical eyes. Looking in the mirror day to day, I didn't really see much of a difference, but I think that was also a case of seeing what I had become accustomed to seeing. For whatever reason, today I saw fully all I'd achieved. I looked fabulous. Even better, I looked fabulous in size 8, something I had never even dared dream possible. I hadn't been a size 8 since elementary school. My little voice piped up to remind me about vanity sizing.

"Shut up and let me enjoy this."

"What was that, honey?" Jarom called from outside the fitting room.

"Oh, um, just asking you to bring more clothes. Mediums if you please."

So Jarom became my pack mule for the day as I schlepped him around from store to store. The world of retail delights was now open to me. I could visit stores that I never dared venture to before because they didn't cater to plus-size girls. But I was no longer a plus-size girl. I took great joy in being frustrated at Dressbarn when the dress that I wanted only had sizes 10 and 14 left. That had never happened before. Sure, plenty of times a store didn't have my size, but it was usually because all the sizes were far too small, not too big. It was the best time I'd had in ages.

I realize most of my friends would be horrified at being a size 8. That's what happens when you surround yourself with bunches of people who are size 2s. Whenever we would go out as the group, I was the big friend. Now when we go out, I'm still the big friend, but only slightly.

Perhaps this running thing was going to be worth it after all. Already in the few months of training, I had learned things that countless hours and dollars spent at therapists hadn't managed to teach me. My eyes were opening to a whole new world of possibilities in what I could wear and what I could be. If my body on the outside was changing for the better, then the me on the inside could change for the better too.

5

WHO SAYS TV *isn't* EDUCATIONAL?

Jarom's and my weekly running schedule consisted of four runs—a short, a medium, another short, and a long (usually two to three times the distance of the short). On days when there was no school and no one to watch the kids, we turned running in the cold into a family affair. In truth, the kids actually enjoyed our runs. I mean, who wouldn't enjoy being chauffeured around in a cushy double stroller with toys, snacks, and drinks. Jarom, in his infinite wisdom, decided that since I was the one trying to lose weight, I should be the one to push the stroller. Burn more calories he claimed. Hmmm . . . yeah right.

One particular Saturday in March, the schedule called for a five-mile run, which equaled about eight laps around the long track at the park. Headphones in, music pumping, Jarom beside me and stroller in front of me, I started my run. Jarom concentrated on proper running form and left me in charge of the girls. So I pushed the seventy-five pounds of two kids plus the stroller over the rolling hills, the entire time thinking I got the raw end of the deal.

Four laps and half an hour later, I swear the stroller gained an extra fifty pounds. What toys had Jarom given the kids? Bricks? So I huffed and puffed up to the nearest oasis, the park bench. I set the locking brake on the stroller, pulled out my headphones, and collapsed on the cold, hard metal.

Lily popped her head out of the blanket she had been under. "Whatcha doin', Mommy?"

"I'm taking a break. You guys weigh a ton!" I looked around to pass the stroller off to Jarom, but he was "conveniently" on the other side of the park.

"Are you out of en-jury, Momma?"

"Yes, Lily, Momma's out of energy"

Lily seemed to be thinking long and hard about something. After a moment, she dug deep into her pack and pulled out a small baggie of cookies. "Here, Momma, eat these. They will give you en-jury."

My wonderful Lily was good at many things, but sharing was not one of them. Something must have been going on in her little head for her to offer her prized snack with me. When I said no, thank you, she looked both relieved at not having to part with her treat and upset that I wasn't taking them.

"But you gotta cuz you need mo' en-jury to keep going." She pushed the bag of cookies into my hand.

"Aren't you ready to go home yet? We could quit a little early just for today, and then I'll make you some hot cocoa."

"Nope, no quitting. Gabba Gabba says 'Keep trying, keep trying. Don't give up. Never give up.' So I will sing the song for you, then you will finish your race with Daddy, and then you will make me hot chocat. K?"

And she did just that. The song she was talking about was from one of her favorite Nickelodeon TV shows *Yo Gabba Gabba*. Previously I had questioned the wisdom in letting her watch that show—it was really weird. But if they were teaching her this, it couldn't be that bad.

As we went around the track four more times, she repeated the only three lines of the songs she remembered.

Keep trying, Keep trying

Don't give up, Never give up

Don't stop, Don't give up

Over and over again ad naseum and off key. I'm not sure which motivated me to run faster, her words of encouragement or her shrill singing, but I finished in record time. Lily beamed up at me, so proud of our accomplishment.

"Yay for Mommy. . . . Can I have my cookies back now?"

My four-year-old put me to shame that day, and made me think long and hard about how I had been approaching this adventure. So far I'd been running, putting in my time, and enjoying the weight-loss benefits without actually believing I would run a marathon. But now I wondered. What if Jarom didn't quit? Did I even want him to? Could I have any hope of success when I had been planning on failing all along? Then my thoughts drifted toward my daughters and the kind of example I was setting for them. Did I want them to grow up thinking like me? That when things got hard, it was better to quit than fail?

I had picked up my bad habit of not finishing from my mom. She claimed that "The end is boring; it's the beginning that's more fun." She's always starting new projects and finding new hobbies. She found her niche raising guide-dog puppies. It was the perfect pursuit for her because she loves the beginning when they're puppies but isn't a big fan of dogs when they get big and aren't cute and fluffy anymore. So she trains them for a year, then gives them back and gets a new one. Perpetual fuzzy happiness.

That may work for her, but I had grown weary off all my starts. While my mom viewed each thing she didn't finish as something that no longer deserved her time, I saw my unfinished business as failures. Each time I gave up, I envisioned myself laying a brick in a wall that had slowly grown over time until I was surrounded and trapped within it. I couldn't find my way out. I couldn't see past this giant wall I'd built with all my failures staring back at me. But every time I finished a run, a brick disappeared, opening a small window, allowing the light into the dark places of my psyche.

I wanted more holes, and shorter walls to climb, so I promised not to give up on myself again. I made Lily her hot cocoa and gave her three extra marshmallows and a kiss on the head.

"I got lots of mellows! How come?"

"'Cause you're so smart, Lil."

***

Of course, promising not to quit proved a whole lot easier in theory than in practice. My first real test came two weeks later during a spring storm. Jarom and I were trying to get our medium run in before work that morning. The girls were at preschool, so it was just the two of us and about fifty thousand drops of rain. Since our runs got progressively longer each week of training, our medium run was now the length of the long a few weeks ago. Five miles in the rain. Fun, fun.

It started off lightly drizzling, and since we had on rain gear, it wasn't too bad. The water rolled off the slick surface and kept us dry. But did you know that water resistant is not the same as waterproof? When I purchased the jackets, I didn't know that there was a difference, but I did now. At three miles, our "weather resistant" jackets hit their water limit. Right as the light pecks of rain turned into giant slobbery dog kisses.

Everything was wet. The jacket, the turtleneck under the jacket, the bra under the—you get the point. Worst of all, though, were the wet shoes and socks.

"What is that sound?" Jarom asked.

"What sound?" I replied much louder since I still had my earphones in.

Jarom shook his head and pulled the earphones out of my ears. Still running, we listened quietly for a moment until I heard the noise over my chattering teeth.

"Oh, the squishy squish noise? Those are my socks."

"Seriously?"

"Yup."

Jarom stopped and grabbed my elbow to halt my momentum. "I think three and a half miles is good enough for today. What do you say?"

Oooh, it was tempting. I wanted to go home and stand under a hot shower for an hour. I could hear it calling my name from three blocks away. But I could also hear Lily's singing in the back of my head too. I had promised to not quit again, so how would I feel if I left now without finishing? Warm, true. But also like I had proven to myself once again that I was useless and couldn't so something I'd promised to do. I thought to myself, *Come on Bets, it's only another mile and a half. You can do that easy.* (How crazy was it that a mile and a half was now small potatoes when a few months ago running to the mailbox was agony?)

I popped my earphones back in and said loudly, "You can go back if you want, but I'm gonna finish." With a squish-squish, I was on my way again.

Chivalry is not dead, because Jarom trotted after me, though he was muttering under his breath the whole time. It was hard to make out over my music, so I'll give him the benefit of the doubt by saying it sounded like, "Got dandruff, and some of it itches."

Over the last mile and a half, I had no trouble keeping up positive thoughts. Pride was a relatively new emotion to me, so it took me a few minutes to separate it from my shivering. I was actually proud myself. Even though I was miserable, cold, wet, and hungry, I kept my promise and kept moving. I remembered the mantra I was supposed to repeat and said it with conviction. Dang, I can do it, and I am awesome.

I tried smiling at Jarom encouragingly, but I only got scowls in return. Apparently he was not totally down with my no-quitting plan. With some time and a warm blanket, I'm sure he would come around . . . eventually.

An unintended bonus of running in the rain was that it made everything else seem like cake. The evil little voice still piped up and told me I was too tired or sore to get out of bed and run. But experience reminded me how miserable it had been running with squishy shoes and a few sore muscles were nothing in comparison. Eventually it became automatic and unquestioning. If a run was on the schedule, I would go and get it done. No struggle, no worries, no dilemma. This no-quitting thing was actually making my life easier! Who knew?

***

I had proved to myself that I could overcome physical discomfort and push onward, but what would I do in the face of social and emotional discomfort? I had the opportunity to find out at my first Zumba class.

For anyone who doesn't know, Zumba is a fitness dance class taught at many gyms and rec centers. It's a high-intensity cardio mix of Latin and hip-hop dance styles. Supposedly you could burn up to one thousand calories in an hour. Ooh, that sounded good to me. My head was filled with visions of all the treats I could eat with all those extra calories burned.

I have to admit that I had a bit of a peacock complex at this point. I was a runner (sort of), and a musician to boot, so logic told me that I would nail this since I had the endurance and rhythm taken care of. I walked into class in my spiffy little cargo pants and tank top, ready to bust a move. I busted all right, just not in a good way. Looking back at myself in that giant floor-to-ceiling mirror, let me tell you, white girl can't dance. While my head and fingers understood the rhythm, my feet and hips found themselves trying to speak a foreign language.

Ten minutes in, I wanted to go home. This was incredibly embarrassing. I was incapable of following along and copying the dance steps. Nobody showed you the steps beforehand; you were just supposed to pick it up by watching everyone else. Well, my eyes and my feet were not communicating properly, because I couldn't duplicate what I was seeing. When the room grapevined left, I grapevined right, causing a head-on collision with the lady next to me. I snuck out of the room in the guise of needing a drink from the water fountain.

I took forever to walk back, debating with myself the whole way. Could I leave now? I had tried it and I didn't like it. That wasn't the same thing as giving up, was it? Maybe it was technically quitting. There had to be a loophole in the no-quitting promise I made. Surely there was an out clause if you really and truly sucked at it. I paused outside the glass door and looked at the twenty or so women inside.

Watching the teacher, I was pretty sure you had to be a professional dancer to make your body sway that way. I looked around at the other ladies in the room, shaking what their mama gave them. A few managed to duplicate the teacher's smooth hip rolls, but the others just jiggled their . . . (um, how to be diplomatic?) . . . rotund rear ends. (Note: It's not only rude to stare at other people's butts during class, but it can also cause nightmares.)

Didn't these women know that they looked silly? Judging from their faces, I would say no. They were actually smiling! Why? This was hard. I couldn't remember which foot went where, my lefts and rights consistently the opposite of everyone else in the room. Several women in the room were natural dancers with the accompanying little body, but the majority of them were just like me—middle-aged moms trying to keep the fat at bay.

There was one woman in the back of the room that caught my attention. She was probably in her mid-sixties with short gray hair and an oversized T-shirt that I think read "Groovin' Granny." (My glasses weren't on and she was wiggling too much.) Her steps were always a beat or two behind the others, and her arms flailed every which way. Dancing was clearly not her forte, but she was having the time of her life.

I don't know if it was determination not to quit or shame at being outdanced by a woman twice my age, but I went back into the class, ready to try again. The spot next to Granny was open, so I took it. Later I realized that it was open because no one wanted to stand next her and get smacked by her helicopter-like arms.

At one point in class, I was standing still, utterly lost, when Granny smacked me in the chest.

"Oh sorry, dear. Hey, if you're having trouble just jump around and keep moving. Nobody will notice the difference." Then she went back to her spastic movements.

I decided to give her advice a try. After all, that's what you did when you forgot words to a song—mouth the word *watermelon* until you remembered. Fake it till you make it, baby. For the rest of class, I gave up trying to salsa and shimmy like a samba dancer and just gyrated in the same general direction as everyone else. It was surprisingly liberating. By the end of class, I was only slightly frustrated at my lack of choreography skills.

I approached the teacher after class so she could show me one of the basic steps that was repeated often and always tripped me up. She gladly showed me and then lied shamelessly, telling me I had done really well for a first-timer.

"Come back next week. It gets easier, I promise."

Yeah, sure it did. I spent the next week debating whether to return to class. On one hand, I enjoyed feeling the music through physical expression. On the other, my physical expression was anything but harmonious. In the end, I decided that I wanted to learn how to dance more than I was self-conscious of my lack of skill. I went back Tuesday night, and almost every Tuesday after, even to the point that I am writing this.

Did I ever master the merengue? Nope, I'm still awful, but it is my absolute favorite part of the week. There's a freedom in looking at yourself and saying, "Yes, I may look silly, but I'm having a blast and don't care who sees me."

***

At the time, I didn't fully grasp what the no-quitting pledge was doing for me. I wasn't planning to change my life; I was just trying to prove to myself and to my family that I could keep my promises. That when I said I was going to do something, I would do it. They were just little things, a run here or a project there. The outcome of the task itself was not earth shattering. Running the full five miles instead of just three and a half did not hugely alter my life. I'm positive it would have made almost zero difference in my training and ability to run the marathon.

The real difference occurred within me. Each success motivated me to do more, to keep that happy feeling for a little bit longer. It also built a confidence in myself that I hadn't really had before. I could do things now that I'd quit on previously—because now I knew that I was capable of it. It wasn't just faith that I could. I had proof. Each little thing that I didn't quit on began to stack itself neatly into a little pile in the corner of my mind. That pile grew and became the evidence that I can show myself when times get tough. Now when my little voice says, "You're nobody. You can't do anything," I can point to my evidence and say, "Yes, I can. Look at all these things I didn't quit on." It keeps me going and gives me the courage to try to go farther and higher than I let myself go before.

Unwittingly, by not quitting, I had created a group of tangible accomplishments. And it continues to grow. It's probably one of the few things I don't mind expanding. I want—no, I need—that pile to grow until it's the size of a mountain. Then I could use it to stand on and peer over the wall of failures I had erected. There was a whole world to discover outside of that little failure room I'd bricked myself into. All I needed was the courage to climb out.

6

IF YOU'RE STILL ALIVE *at* the END *of* the DAY, YOU'RE *a* SUCCESS

I've always struggled with the feeling that who I was wasn't enough, that everyone around me was better or more successful than I was. It felt like I had somehow strayed from the path to that bright future I had foreseen as a child, and now I was embarrassed by what I was—a stay-at-home mom.

Facebook is the high school reunion that never ends. You can tell how popular you are by how many "friends" you have. The popular kids will still "ignore" your existence. And you will still compare your looks to your first love's significant other. At least at the real ten-year reunion you can lie about being successful for a night. It's a whole lot harder to fake it 24/7 with the whole Internet watching. But I didn't think about any of that when my sister lured me onto Facebook a few years ago.

Seemed harmless enough, right? It was a convenient way to keep up with close family and friends that lived out of state. I didn't realize that everybody and their dog were on Facebook. That people I hadn't seen or talked to in fifteen years would request to be my friend. That I would now have to account for what I had done or not done since high school.

When the first former classmate found me, I was embarrassed to admit that no, I hadn't gone on to be a big shot musician, just a stay-at-home mom. Nope, never did finish that four-year degree. What was going on in my life? Um, pretty much nothing. I felt like I was being measured against some standard and falling horribly short. Well, nothing a little creative editing couldn't fix. I believe politicians call it spin.

I scoured my computer for hours, trying to find a decent photo of me from one of my diet successes that I could use as a profile picture. (Hey, nobody said the photo had be current.) Then I went to work on the "info" portion of my user account.

Favorite Quotes: I searched the web and cut and pasted ones that made me sound deep and well read.

Favorite Music: I made sure to leave out any guilty pleasures ("Mmmbop" wasn't going to cut it) and only included music that would reflect favorably on my musical background like classical and Broadway.

Occupation: I went from stay-at-home mom to writer. (It wasn't a lie since at the time I was fifty pages into my latest attempt at a novel.)

Education: I listed myself as having graduated with a liberal arts degree. Nobody else needed to know that it was an associate's and not a bachelor's degree.

Omission was the name of the game. I knew that I wasn't a success, but nobody else had to.

One of the things that you may have noticed as a common theme in my life was my own belief that I was a nobody. I had done nothing of import, nothing noteworthy. I had nothing to show for my years on this earth. Where was the giant plaque that would say "I was here . . . I did this"? Since I didn't have one, I figured I must not be a success.

I viewed my life in terms of the things I hadn't done, rather than giving myself credit for the things I had done. If I was going to find any sort of peace within myself, then that needed to change. And it did . . . so subtly at first that I didn't even know it.

***

When Jarom and I started running, I looked at it in terms of the big picture. I was training for a marathon. One that I was sure was never going to happen, but I was putting in my best effort anyway. The marathon was the goal, the event. Everything leading up to it was just the little details. Running my very first mile got maybe a two-sentence notice from me.

As Jarom and I were walking home, I said, "Well, that was the first mile I have ever run. I always walked them in PE."

"Good job, baby."

"Yeah, but it was hard. I don't know how we're supposed to run two on Wednesday."

Jarom grunted and we slugged on home. Looking back, I want to take a time machine and smack myself. When we had started running, all I could manage before keeling over was five minutes. We were so bad we had to train just to work up to the start of the training schedule. And now after that, I had just run my first mile, and all I could focus on was that there was more to come. How about taking a minute to say, "Oh my gosh. I ran a whole mile. Last week I could run ten steps, but look at how much farther I've come." But no, not me. I had to look at how much farther I had to go.

At the conclusion of each run, the conversation was nearly identical. "Yep, we ran x miles, but on Saturday we have to run y miles." That went on until our first four-mile run.

You have to remember that I went into this whole running thing with the expectation that we would be quitting any day now. I had given us two weeks max before Jarom petered out, so I never expected to reach a third week and a four-mile long run. I don't know what it was, I'm not tetraphobic (fear of the number four), but for some reason my mind balked at the thought of completing four miles. It was impossible, and I was sure the fabric of reality would unravel if I actually did it.

I approached that morning run with as much trepidation and fear as I would a poisonous snake.

"Are you ready?" Jarom asked, lacing up his shoes.

"No."

"Are you going to be ready?"

"No."

"Good, then I guess I get a head start." And the little bugger took off.

What a jerk! Couldn't he see this was hard for me? A good husband would have taken my hand and run around the track with me. An even better husband would have walked me home instead. But no, my husband was a butt-head. Well if he wanted a race, then I would give him one.

I passed him around mile two, but that wasn't good enough for me. I was now dead set on trying make his humiliation complete by lapping him. Focused and pushing myself harder, I had completely forgotten my earlier worries. I wasn't thinking in terms of miles, just how many laps I had left before my victory was assured.

When I made the required laps to equal four miles (we counted and measured ahead of time), I did a victory dance that would have put any footballer to shame. I didn't manage to lap Jarom, but I was far enough ahead of him that I had time to sit down, stretch, and pretend to take a nap. When he finally got there, I congratulated him like the good sport I was.

"Ha! I kicked your butt. You weren't even close. Teach you to try and race me. You cheated and *still* lost." I probably said a few other choice phrases, but I'm embarrassed enough for one chapter.

When Jarom finally caught his breath, "Yep, you sure did. You ran the whole four miles. Didn't have to walk once."

It hit me like a running shoe to the head: I had run four miles. I had done the impossible, and just like I had predicted, the fabric of reality unraveled . . . I actually gave myself credit. For once, I was in the moment of the achievement, not looking ahead at how much more I had to do. Or looking at how long it had taken me to do it. (Even though I was faster than Jarom, I was still pretty slow.) Nope, for once I was able to appreciate the simple fact that I had done something.

Earlier animosity forgotten, I grabbed Jarom in huge bear hug. Then I started a new, better victory dance.

"I ran four miles. *I ran four miles.* I am a goddess!" Hey, I didn't say I was humble about it. Baby steps.

***

My bedroom has a set of his and her IKEA wardrobes. On the doors of the wardrobes were three calendar pages, one for the current month and the following two months. Using a book (what else?), Jarom had come up with a training schedule that worked for us and put it on the calendars so we could easily track how far we were running on what days. It had been intended as a tool to help us plan ahead and arrange our schedule accordingly. My four-year-old, Lily, saw it differently.

One day, she came into our room as I was checking off that morning's run.

"Hey, Mama, is that your sticker card?"

"Huh? What're you talking about, Lily?"

Lily ran out of the room and brought back the reward chart that I had made for her earlier that week. We had recently been having a little trouble with naughty behavior in our household. Lily had been seeing an occupational therapist for the past six months for sensory processing issues. The therapist had suggested the reward chart as a way to not only encourage positive behavior but also recognize it. Every time Lily did a good job at following directions, shared with her sister, or didn't flip out when she put on her shoes (long story), she got a sticker in one of the boxes. When she filled up a row with stickers, she got a prize. Looking at her paper, I understood why she made the connection. It too was gridded and blocked similarly to the weeks on my calendar.

I looked at my schedule in an entirely new way. Instead of seeing how many more miles I had to go, I looked back at all the check marks showing the miles I'd run. Holy crap, that was a lot of miles. Cumulatively equaling 172 at this point.

"Yes, Lily, this is Mommy's sticker chart."

Lily once again ran out of the room. This time she returned with a page of metallic star stickers.

"You forgot the stickers. Can I do it?"

"Sure, Lily. Just make sure you don't cover up the numbers so I can see how far I went, okay?"

Hoisting Lily up so she could reach, we put little star stickers on each run I'd completed. I'm sure if I had let her have free reign, she would have filled up all the future boxes too. We stood back and admired our handiwork.

"Wow, Mom, that's a lot of stickers. So what's your prize?"

Haha . . . if only. I tried to figure out how to explain to my little girl that grown-ups didn't get rewards. Then I started thinking, Why the heck shouldn't I get a prize? I've earned it!

"I don't know, Lily. Why don't you go ask Daddy?"

I chuckled as Lily ran from the room, yelling for her Daddy the entire way. A few minutes later, she came panting back.

"Daddy says it's whatever."

I'm not sure if Jarom meant whatever I wanted or more likely had no clue what Lily was talking about and so responded with a "Whatever." I decided to use my new powers of positive thinking and believe it was the former. The pants I had bought for my birthday a month ago had gotten a little roomy. Perhaps a little trip to the mall was in order. I looked again at my "sticker chart." Yep, I totally deserved it.

***

My newfound powers of observation didn't belong solely to my running. Nope, it leaked into my everyday life as well. Let me warn you that I'm altering names and a few key details to protect the not-so-innocent. I was at a friend's wedding reception, staring longingly at the gourmet cupcakes when I was tapped on the shoulder.

"Is that you, Betsy? It's me. Stacey Jones. Well, now it's Stacey Adams. You look uh-mazing! How the heck are you?" She then accosted me with a hug.

inward sigh Yes, I recognized my former classmate's voice before she gave her name. With an ear for music and pitch, I had excellent voice recognition. It's a curse. Cue fake smile.

"Stacey . . . so good to see you. I didn't know you were friends with the bride."

"Oh, no. I'm the groom's cousin."

Of course, for all the rotten luck. Remember a couple of chapters ago, when I mentioned that I left the music behind in college because of some of the criticism I received. Well, a large portion of that had come from the woman standing in front of me now.

She grabbed me with her manicured claws and dragged me off to a table where she could devour me in private.

"So fill me in. What happened after you left school? Did you ever finish your degree?"

It was tempting to lie about it or give my omitted Facebook answer. Instead I owned up to the truth, the whole truth.

"You know what? I managed to get my associate's in liberal arts and then got busy and never got around to finishing."

"Oh, that's too bad. But if you were too busy to finish, you must have had something great going on. Did you get a big job or a gig playing somewhere?"

Okay, was somebody giving this lady cue cards or cheat sheets of all my buttons to push for maximum insecurity?

"Nope, I just got busy with life. Got married, had a few kids. Girls. One of them's a real handful, and she keeps me pretty occupied."

"Oh. Well, I got married too, see?" She blinded me with the oversized gem weighing down her claw. "But no kids yet. There just isn't time with Jim being a doctor and my master's program. How did you find time with your career? What did you say you did again?"

I could have given her the author line or tried to make myself sound more accomplished and important, but for once, I didn't feel the need.

Everything about her was trying to scream "I'm better than you." From her huge diamond, designer clothes, and casual dropping of her husband's profession, all of it was too in your face. It was a calculated attempt to make her seem bigger and badder than she was. She reminded me of a blowfish, prickly and full of hot air.

I had nothing to prove to this woman. After this torturous conversation, we would go our separate ways and, God willing, never meet again. I didn't need her approval of my life. I only needed my own. With a start, I realized that I had it, at least on some of the most basic levels. Sure, I still looked in the mirror and bemoaned my skinny rolls. (I didn't have fat rolls any more, just the loose flaps of skin left over from losing sixty-five pounds.) I still kicked myself on occasion if I felt I could've done better. But I had come to see that the woman I'd become was an accomplishment in its own right.

I had the hardest job on the planet. I was a stay-at-home mom. Two little lives depended on me. I was responsible for making sure they ate nutritious foods, stayed clean, got enough sleep, learned right from wrong, used their manners, stayed in bed when they were sick, and most important, felt that they were loved. I was a housekeeper, a short-order cook (drive-thrus count), nurse, teacher, spiritual leader, and entertainer all rolled into one.

And I didn't get to clock out at the end of the day either. Being a mother never ends. Who else would wake up in the middle of the night and clean up vomit, then stay up with them the rest of the night, bowl at the ready. By the end of the day, my girls were alive and hopefully a little better and a little smarter than they were the day before. Me too. If that didn't make me feel like a success, then nothing else I did ever would.

I didn't actually say that entire rant out loud, though I probably should have. Instead I proudly proclaimed my profession and made my exit.

"I'm a stay-at-home mom. Worst paying job in the world, but the perks are amazing. Now if you'll excuse me, I should get home to my two little perks about now. Lovely catching up with you. Good luck on your school. I'm sure you'll graduate and get to be a mom soon."

I got up and left her flabbergasted by my abrupt and slightly rude departure. I was pleased with myself both for the personal revelations about my everyday accomplishments and for the restraint I showed by not bashing her head with the vase. I had faced down a demon, not Stacey, per se, but more accurately the feeling that I needed to be ashamed and apologize for who I had become. For probably the first time I could look at my life with a sense of accomplishment for what it was instead of a sense of loss for what I wished it would have been.

7

WHEN SHARING *a* DESSERT, ALWAYS ASSUME *that* 90 PERCENT *of the* CALORIES ARE *in the* OTHER PERSON'S HALF

can't lie convincingly to another person, and I can't play poker to save my life, but I am a master at self-deception. I could fool myself into thinking I was on the right track when in fact I was going the wrong way on a one-way street. That was one of the reasons my diet efforts always failed, because I lied to myself about how much I was really eating. Sure I counted calories. I knew one portion of Chex mix was 140; I just ignored the fact that their portion was a quarter cup and my portion was half the bag. But in my little food journal, I faithfully wrote down my one portion of Chex mix and patted myself on the back for my excellent tracking skills.

Now that I was measuring every darned thing that went into my mouth, I could see how ridiculous my behavior had been. I had put blinders on to everything that didn't gel with what I wanted. Sometimes, I knew I'd done wrong and feel guilty about it, but most of the times I talked myself into actually believing the BS I made up to excuse my actions. Here are a few of my favorite food lies and myths that I used shamelessly.

1. **You don't have to count the calories if you are picking off someone else's plate.**

I am a forever eating off my kids' plates. They eat like birds, and there is something about a mostly untouched plate of food that I find morally offensive. I just paid five bucks for those nuggets and fries and, gosh darnit, somebody was going to enjoy it. Did I add it to my daily food tally? No, they ordered it, so they could pick up the caloric tab.

2. **Dropped food has no caloric value.**

It's like the five-second rule. You choose to believe that there are no germs on that piece of food you just dropped. I choose to believe that the calories fell off on impact with the ground.

3. **Milk chocolate is in the dairy food group**

Says it right there in the name, doesn't it? And you're supposed to have three servings a day. My size servings.

4. **You don't have to count the calories in anything you add to vegetables to make them taste good.**

Because that would be mean to make me eat brussels sprouts and then penalize me for the pound of butter I had to put on them.

5. **When sharing a dessert, always assume that 90 percent of the calories are in the other person's half.**

After all you don't know how those ingredients got dispersed in baking. I'm sure my husband's half soaked up all the caramel.

Now I laugh at the absurdity of these claims (although I still think the chocolate one makes sense), but I totally bought into them at the time. A few years ago, the doctor told me to keep a food journal so we could figure out where all my unwanted pounds were coming from. When I came back a month later and two pounds heavier, he was as mystified as I was since my journal was the picture of healthy eating. When he implied that I must be cheating, I was outraged. How dare he! Why on earth would I cheat? I was the one that came to him, after all. I had written

down everything I had made myself at mealtimes. I'm sure I wasn't supposed to write down the bite or two from the unfinished plates. That
wasn't my food, and I wrote down all of my food. So I didn't cheat, I
must be a medical marvel. I was just destined to be fat, I guess, because it
couldn't be my fault.

And that's what it boiled down to. I lied to myself, rationalizing my
actions so that they fell within the rules. And if I followed the rules, it
couldn't be my fault, right? Something, or someone else, was to blame for
my unhappiness, not little old me.

It wasn't just lying about food, though. When I looked at other things
I'd failed at, I found a whole slew of excuses I used to make myself feel
better about quitting. Stop me if these sound familiar.

1. I can't be skinny like the other girls because I'm big boned.

An oldie but a goodie. It's not my fault I'm fat; I was just built this
way. It has absolutely nothing to do with the fact that I just ate my meal
plus Lily's plus the doggie bag from Jarom's meal.

2. I can't exercise because I'm not athletic.

I've been knocked out by a goal post, a volleyball, and a tennis racket
(all true). Clearly I am not the type of person made for sports, so I should
just stay on the couch, where it's safe.

3. My house is only messy because I'm really busy.

My day is scheduled down to the minute. And yes, that includes the
time I'm sitting on the couch, reading a book, or watching TV. This six-
hour marathon of *Friends* will not watch itself.

4. I haven't quit. I'm only taking a break.

Everybody needs a sabbatical now and then. Scrapbook paper doesn't
have an expiration date. Sure the kids might be twenty-five by the time I
get back around to their scrapbooks, but it'll still get done.

5. I'm not very good at it, so I shouldn't waste my time on it.

Because I'm sure that all the musicians in the world were born with
that kind of talent and didn't have to practice for years to get that good.
And my time is precious (see number three).

Now that the only thing I was giving up was quitting, the excuses
rang hollow and untrue in my ears. One by one, I was proving them

wrong. While it's true I'm taller and broader than the average woman, the amount of fat I stored (a whopping forty-five percent body fat) had a whole lot less to do with genetics than with the pint of Ben and Jerry's I ate when I got depressed.

Now that I was counting calories and controlling portion sizes, the fat was disappearing. I had debunked the big-boned myth. Running helped me dispel number two. Don't get me wrong, I am still not an athlete. I routinely trip over my running shoes, but that doesn't mean I can't go out and do it anyway. Numbers three and four were pretty obvious once I started being honest with myself.

But number five took a little bit of work and a whole lot longer to get over. Some days I still get stuck in this trap. My aim in life has always been to be the best at whatever I do. That's an admirable goal, but I took it to the extreme. Anything but the best resulted in failure. So when it appeared that I was not going to master something, I'd quit, thinking that stopping was better than failure. I was not in control of my life. I swayed whatever way the wind blew. If I wasn't good at something, then fate must have decreed that it wasn't to be. I didn't want to take responsibility for the choices that led to my failures. My unhappiness couldn't be my fault— stuff just happened to me and kept me from my dreams.

***

Jarom had his heart set on running the St. George Marathon. Growing up, when he saw himself running a marathon, that was the one he envisioned. It's supposed to be one of the most beautiful races in the country with the red rock and sandstone cliffs of Zion National Park in the backdrop. And that's why everyone else wants to run it too. Upwards of 20,000 racers are vying for 7,400 spots. (Yes, I think its crazy too that this many people want to kill themselves running in the desert.) Registration opens up each year only during April. Anyone who signs up and pays the entry fee will be entered in the computerized lottery. The winners are posted the second week of May.

This made for a tense month of April. We signed up on the first day of registration, then we waited. I was really nervous, and I had no idea which result I was rooting for. If we made it into the race, then we had the pressure of being registered and paid for a marathon I didn't think we could run. This made the possibility of failure much more real. On the other hand, if we weren't selected, then we could always say "Well, we tried. We'll try again next year." Then it wouldn't directly be our fault that we didn't meet our goal; the blame would be diverted to the stupid computers. But let's be honest, what are the odds that we would still be running in a year?

In the meantime, we ran and discussed what we were going to do.

"So what's the plan?"

"Plan for what?" Jarom wheezed.

"Plan B if we don't make the cut."

"I'm sure we'll get in."

"But what if we don't?"

Jarom stopped to take a swig of water before replying. "Then I don't know."

"You don't know? This whole thing was your idea! You don't have a backup plan, and we might have been running these last two months for nothing?" I squeaked, horrified.

Jarom chuckled. "So now you're saying you want to run a marathon."

"No, I'm saying it's really stupid to have put forth all this effort on the off chance we would make it in."

"Okay, smartie pants, then what's your backup plan?"

"Humph. I'll get back to you on that." More chuckling from the peanut gallery.

I didn't have a plan either. I was too conflicted. We'd been telling our friends and family that we were training for a marathon. Everyone knew what we were attempting to do. Most of them thought we were crazy, myself included. I felt the pressure of everyone's gaze, watching whether or not we would actually complete our goal. I dreaded the prospect of telling people when they asked that we had not in fact run a marathon—that we'd given up. But what if when people asked I could honestly say, "We entered St. George but weren't selected, so we'll try again another year." It was an excuse, but one that would probably spare us a good deal of embarrassment later on.

I waffled back and forth all month until one morning I opened my email and saw the automated message from the race officials. The results were in. I held my breath and double clicked. We're sorry to inform you . . .

That was as far as I got before tears obscured my vision. Why on earth was I crying? Come on. I should be relieved. My easy out had just been handed to me, practically gift-wrapped. I wouldn't have to run a marathon. I could crawl back into my little comfort zone without the threat of impending failure constantly hanging over my head. That was what I wanted, right?

I realized that it wasn't anymore. I didn't want to be the girl that was always offering excuses for the things I didn't do. I wanted to be the woman that tried to run a marathon, whether I could finish it or not. To put myself out there and reach for something more, even when it meant that I would be opening myself up to the possibility of failure. It would be embarrassing if I had to tell people that I didn't finish the marathon, but I felt like it was going to hurt worse if I knew in my heart that I hadn't even tried.

I wanted this. I needed this. If Jarom really wanted to, we would enter the St. George Marathon lottery again next year. But as for this year, I had to find myself a new race. I dried my tears and did a little digging and discovered that Park City (an hour and a half north of us) had a marathon and it still had plenty of spots available, with no lottery. The only problem was the timing. It was a month and a half sooner than the St. George Marathon. If I was already worried whether we would be ready in five months, how were we going to be ready in three and a half? The probability of failure just doubled in my mind. I didn't know what to do. Luckily, I had my running partner that I could consult.

Jarom was pretty sad that we weren't picked to run in the St. George Marathon. I told him about my backup plan, but he wasn't sure. When he dreamt about running a marathon, he saw himself among the picturesque canyons in the south. The thought of running near the ski slopes in the north threw him for a loop. His brain did not want to adjust to the vision I had presented him.

"I don't know, Betsy. It's too soon. And the course is supposed to be harder."

"It is?" Hmmm, my Internet research had not turned up that little bit of information.

"Yes, it is. I looked up a bunch of different races. Park City is supposed to be one of the hardest in the state. Probably not one you want to do for your first marathon."

I was not even going to address the first marathon comment. As if there were going to be a second? Magic eight ball says all signs point to no.

"So did you find any better options?" I asked.

"Nothing in state. Any of the easier courses are scheduled even sooner that the Park City one."

"So you're saying our choices are basically between doing a difficult course before we're ready or putting it off until next year so we have more time to train."

"Yep, pretty much."

"Great. Lovely. So what do you want to do?" I flopped down on the bed defeated.

Jarom patted my shoulder. "I'll leave that up to you. If you really want to run Park City, we'll give it a shot."

Super, I got to decide. So if I picked to run Park City and we weren't ready and didn't finish, then it was my fault. But if I picked next year, that meant I would have to keep running even longer, something I still didn't really enjoy. Maybe we wouldn't even last long enough to get to next year's races.

Going back a few chapters, you might remember that I have a hard time with choices. I had resolved after the shoe incident to pick whatever I wanted and then deal with the consequences. Even though there were more reasons against than for, I really wanted to run Park City. The cons were the ones we'd already gone over: too soon and tough course. A big pro for me was getting it done while I still had the motivation to do it. I was new to the no-quit pledge, and I didn't know how long it would last.

The other pro was kind of silly and shallow—the finisher medal. Everybody that finished the race in the allotted time got a finisher medal. Park City is a very artsy community, so their finisher medals were unique handmade stained-glass leaves. They were gorgeous, and I wanted one.

"Okay, let's do it," I resolved.

"All right, Park City it is."

I had listened to my own excuses and decided to try anyway. Yes, chances were high that we would fail miserably, but who knew? If we didn't make it, we didn't make it, but at least we would have tried. Not to mention, the chances of getting my pretty finisher medal went up dramatically if we actually entered.

***

I was finally taking responsibility for my life and my actions. I think that up to this point I had been a passenger on the road of life, plodding along in some junker. And when it inevitably broke down, I would whine about my rotten luck, but what could I do? After all, I was just a passenger, and it wasn't as if I had any control over the things that happened to me.

Seeing myself as a victim of fate, is it any wonder that I was unhappy with the way things were going? Losing the excuses had put me squarely in the driver's seat of what I envisioned as an armored Jeep. I had driven myself to this point in my life. Sure, genetics definitely played a part, but

I think the empty pizza boxes spoke a lot louder about the choices I had been making that led me to the thud.

For me, taking responsibility is not a matter of blame but of control. As a passenger, I had no control over my life. Living in constant worry waiting for the other shoe to drop was not healthy for my mind or my indigestion. Bad things happened, and there was nothing I could do about it. I hate that feeling of helplessness. Always looking over my shoulder, waiting for something to push me down. It took consciously choosing what I believed about myself and my relationship with the world. Was there some predestined life that I was supposed to lead and I just had to bear the rough patches? Or did I decide what I would do and who I would be?

I chose to believe that while yes, some things happen for a reason, one of those reasons was that I make it happen. As a driver, I decide which way I am going to go and how I let things affect me. Sure it means that I have to take ownership for my "accidents," but it also means that I do not have to sit idly by waiting for a Mack truck to sideswipe me. And just like my car in real life, the driver not only gets to pick the radio station, but she picks the final destination.

better than somebody, and that poor somebody happened to be Jarom.

Over the next two months we trained, and I focused on pushing myself harder until I could literally run laps around Jarom. And bless his heart, he bore it with a grace that I know I couldn't have mustered. Before long I was running faster, breaking the ten-minute per mile average on short runs. Jarom, on the other hand, seemed to be getting slower. His calf began giving him trouble, at first sporadically, but soon became a constant running companion, causing him to cut crucial training runs short.

At first, I'm ashamed to say, I was annoyed. Here I was busting my butt for his dream, and he was sitting on the sidelines. In my head, I was telling him to "Cowboy up." If I could force myself to run through knee pain, then he could get over his calf problems. Then he started skipping one or two runs a week. No longer annoyed, I was worried that he wouldn't be able to run in the half marathon at all. Running by myself wasn't much fun, and that was just the training runs. The prospect of having to run my first race alone was terrifying. Just like that, I no longer cared who came in last, or how many minutes faster than Jarom I would be.

My plans of breezing ahead and then waiting at the finish line were gone. I was seriously concerned that if I left his side, he wouldn't have the support he needed to finish. Well, I was going to be there for him, and I would drag him across the finish if I had to. I remember going to sleep the night before the half marathon thinking it was a good thing I'd been lifting weights in case I had to carry him.

***

On June 11, race day, we forced ourselves out of bed at the ungodly time of 3:30 so we could catch the 4:30 bus to starting line. Between the adrenaline and cold temperatures, I was hopping out of my skin. I was anxious that I would do or say the wrong thing and utterly embarrass myself. The night before had been plagued with nightmares, dreams of being confronted, then turned away by world-class athletes because Jarom and I were too slow and obviously didn't belong. I even had the quintessential dream of showing up naked and having everyone laugh at me.

Fifteen minutes after getting off the bus, I realized I had been flipping out over nothing. At the starting line, the race organizers set up fire barrels so participants could stay warm in the predawn hours, and with twenty-five hundred people vying to get a spot around a barrel, you get a little close to your neighbor.

8

NEEDING *to* STEP *on* SOMEONE

Running an actual race was the real turning point in my life. It focused me so I could see how all these little changes were growing together to make a big change.

Jarom decided that if we were going to make Park City, then we needed to accelerate our training program. We needed to throw in a practice race to help us prepare. That sounded smart; I was on board for that. My friend's hair school was hosting a three-mile fun run downtown. Apparently that wasn't good enough. He informed me that he was signing us up for the Utah Valley Half Marathon.

"You want to do a practice race and you're gonna pick a thirteen-mile run? That's not practice; that's just as hard as running a full marathon."

"Nope, it's only half as hard."

Honestly, I have no clue what Jarom had against the idea of running a 5K, but somebody needed a reality check. We were barely managing our four-mile runs, and he thought we should run more than three times that amount as practice. He really wanted to push the limits of my budding optimism, didn't he?

I had two problems with the thought of running in a real honest-to-goodness race. (I still refused to call it a practice race.) The first problem was that distance. Thirteen miles is forever long. That would be like running to the freeway from my house. And thirteen was just a rotten number anyway. It's unlucky. People became triskaidekaphobic (fear of the number thirteen) for a reason. Maybe they'd let me do twelve miles and call it good.

The second problem went back to my fears. No, not of thirteen, but the fear of being good enough. Of doing it right, or more accurately, of not doing it right and being laughed at. Maybe I could get from point A to point B, but it took forever. I knew that because Jarom had a spiffy little watch (that required a college degree to operate) that measured your heart rate, time elapsed, and calories burned. Using its internal GPS it could also tell you how far you'd run and what your pace was. Pace is how many minutes it takes someone to run a mile. We were somewhere around a thirteen-minute mile. (There's that number again. I'm going to get a complex.) As a point of reference, my friend Sarah Michelle, the Fat Pack instructor, ran a nine-minute mile. We couldn't run together because she'd have to run backward just to maintain my pace.

So I was slow. I didn't need Jarom's high-tech watch to tell me that. Some people walked faster than we ran. Old people with their dogs passed us on the track. Snails secretly snickered as we went by. It was a constant irritant for me. I didn't want to do something just to be lame at it. What was the point in that? A continual theme of my life: If I can't do it well, I don't want to do it. I was going to get faster. Maybe not Boston Marathon fast, but at least Sarah Michelle fast.

***

One day after a really difficult six-mile run, I'd had it. Aside from the pain in my knees, the only thing I felt was frustration. Using my own less-complicated watch, I'd timed myself at one hour, twelve minutes, and forty-six seconds. That averaged out to about twelve-minute miles, maybe a little faster, but I'm pretty sure that time meant I was still pretty lame. But maybe there was hope. I mean how bad could that be really? Perhaps Sarah Michelle's nine-minute miles were considered fast, so that would make me just average instead of bad. I could work with average.

Icing my aches, I hopped on the Internet to confirm. It was even worse than I'd feared. Not only were twelve-minute miles considered slow, but they weren't even considered running. That inauspicious time put me in the dubious company of joggers. All that time and effort I'd spent working up to six miles, and I couldn't even call myself a runner.

I don't know why the label bugged me so much. To me "jogging" w something you did casually, but "running" was something athletes di And I really wanted to be an athlete. Plus, who's ever heard of a maratho jogger?

I sought out Jarom and braced him for the bad news.

"Turns out anything slower than a ten-minute mile is considere jogging."

His eyebrows arched. "And?"

"And since neither one of us can run a ten-minute mile, then we'r not really running at all. We're jogging." I spit out that last sentence with all the distaste it deserved.

Jarom shrugged. "Humph. Feels like running to me."

"Well, it's not. It's jogging."

"I repeat . . . and?"

Ugh. Was he really this dense or had all the running addled his brain "Obviously it means that we can't do the races."

"Why is that?"

I threw my hands up in exasperation. "Because you can't jog in a race. Even if we finish, we'll be dead last. It'll take us so long nobody will even be at the finish line anymore. Seventy-year-olds will be passing us. People with prosthetic limbs will be passing us."

"Who cares?"

It was too much for me. I was cranky because I still wasn't eating enough food, I was tired and sore from a tough run, and my husband wa being a moron. So I did the only thing I could. I started to cry.

"I care." I gasped out in between hitching breaths "I don't want to lose.

Jarom chuckled even as he gathered me into his embrace. "I'm sorr honey, but did you think you had a shot at winning the race?"

Wiping my nose, I said, "No, that's stupid. I just don't want to be last

"And you won't be; I will. You complain about being slow, but I' always behind you. So don't worry about being last, I'll take care of tha You just worry about getting across the finish line. Okay?"

"Okay."

Unknowingly, Jarom had offered me a lifeline. As long as I beat som one, I wouldn't be a loser. A horrible and unhealthy way to look at i know, but there it was. Looking back, I think it was a case of my s esteem being so poor that I needed to step on someone else to get high Back then, the idea that even finishing the race was a huge accompli ment didn't even occur to me. All that mattered was that I had to

In general, people were nice and super chatty. When I told people that this was our first race, they would infallibly tell me how much we'd love it and how great we'd be. Then they'd go on to regale us with stories of their past triumphs and defeats, sharing their venerable wisdom with the newbies. Whenever the conversation got around to asking about running times and personal bests, I would gently sidestep the question and say, "Since this is our first race, we really just want to finish." A few racers kind of scoffed and suggested we aim higher, but most people were really supportive, assuring us that we could do it. I gave that line so often that I actually started to believe it. Maybe I really didn't care what our time was, or what place we were in, as long as Jarom and I finished it together.

When I gave my answer about finishing to one older lady, she smiled and nodded knowingly. "Ahh, so you're a penguin like me. Just stick to the back of the pack, and you'll be fine. Good luck." Then she wandered off to find the rest of her group. Like her, they had the words "Penguin Pacers" on the backs of their shirts.

A penguin? Thinking I'd just been insulted, I went to complain to Jarom. "I think that lady just called me fat."

"Why? What'd she say?"

"She said I looked like a penguin. So was she talking about being thick in the middle, or do I waddle when I run?

Jarom laughed. "Neither. She was probably referring to your place in the pack. Remember rabbits up front and penguins in back. Come on let's go line up next to the other penguins."

Now that he mentioned it, I did remember reading something about that. In one of the many books Jarom had checked out from the library so he could learn to run, there was a book written by a man named John Bingham, otherwise known as the Penguin. They called him that because he looked like one when he ran I guess. The point was that he became a racing celebrity of sorts, and so the term penguin had become synonymous with a slow runner in the back of the pack, like he was. I supposed there were worse things to be, but still the association didn't sound flattering.

Before I had a chance to ruminate any more on the topic, the loudspeakers blared, giving the countdown to the start. Okay, my legs were warmed up and ready to run. As soon as that gun went off, I . . . would shuffle my way forward toward the start line, trapped in the throng of twenty-five hundred sardines? What? This was not how a race was supposed to start. I'd seen the Olympics, and I imagined that this would be much the same—taking off like a rocket as soon as you heard the shot. Maybe that's what happened way up at the front of the pack, but here in the back, it was like rush-hour traffic. Perhaps that's where the term penguin came from—from the herd of people at the back shuffling from foot to foot, inching their way forward. Heck, we couldn't even see the start line yet. Jarom's fancy watch informed us that from the sound of the shot to when we stepped over the start line was four minutes.

The herd finally started thinning out after the first mile, and I'll admit that I for one was not having fun. To start with, my iPod had died, so I was forced to listen to the inane chattering of two twenty-somethings running (shuffling) next to us. Really I did not want to know about your husband's stress at work and resulting "marital issues." TMI. I was also ticked because Jarom made me toss the box of Tic Tacs I kept in my pocket as a pick-me-up. Too noisy, he said. I said I needed it to drown out Tweedle Dum and Tweedle Dummer over there. He won, and I reluctantly took them out and left them by the roadside.

The most disconcerting thing so far was our speed. Even though I'd been saying I just wanted to finish, a small part of me was still worried about getting a decent time. On the bright side, everybody else was going slowly while trying to get through the logjam. Except that guy running through traffic to get past us slowpokes, but he was probably going to get squished, and wouldn't that screw up his time?

Once we were out in the open and not bottlenecked anymore, we settled into a steady pace, what I like to refer to as Jarom speed. My legs were itching to go faster, and I felt that if I could just open the throttle up, I would fly down the course. Instead, I set my cruise control to Jarom speed and got comfortable. We weren't the slowest, not by a long shot. Sometimes we would pass one of those "Penguin Pacers." I was thrilled that we were passing anyone.

Since I didn't have my tunes, I needed to keep my mind occupied so I wouldn't think about aching legs and how much farther we had to go. Those penguin shirts, combined with the race and Jarom's comment about the front runners being rabbits led me to think about the story of the tortoise and the hare—and where exactly the penguin fit in.

Everybody knows the story, right? The tortoise and the hare have a race. The hare, overconfident, keeps stopping to take a break. The tortoise continues at a solid pace, proving that slow and steady wins the race. There was no penguin in that race, but there were in mine. I figured out the hares were the guys sprinting at the shot, giving everything they had within the first five miles. Sure they made excellent time, but the time they gained in those five miles was lost when they were darn near passing out on the side of the road. We'd run by a few that had petered out and were now being carted off by staff, ending their race.

The tortoises were the racers who kept a steady and maintainable pace throughout the race, never running faster than their legs could sustain. And the penguins? They didn't even know they were in the race. Just like their counterparts in nature, they kept going no matter what to get to the end. Real penguins made a journey to the ocean, crossing hundreds of miles to get the fish because their instincts tell them they have to. If they don't, they'll die. For racing penguins, it's not about the rank in the standings; it's about making it to their ocean, the finish line, because they have to. Run, walk, waddle—it doesn't matter. All that mattered was getting to the end.

These were the thoughts that kept me going through miles nine, ten, eleven, and twelve. Jarom had slowed down since his leg was bothering him, but I stuck by him, because we were penguins, and we were going to finish or die. When he stopped at the final aid station for some water, his legs did not want to get started again. With one mile to go, there was no chance in hades that I was going to let him keel over now. Linking my arm with his, I pulled him forward until his cramps eased and he could resume his gait even if it was lopsided.

I'd love to tell you that we finished arm in arm, but I got a little too excited about a hundred yards from the finish and took off. Two hours, seventeen minutes, and thirty seconds after I started, I crossed the finish line. Apparently Jarom had one last shot of adrenaline too because he finished with a time of 2:17:34, only four seconds behind me.

There are no words to describe the emotions that roiled through me. Anything I say wouldn't come close to explaining what I felt, so I won't even try. What I will say is that the finisher medal they put around my neck could have been Olympic gold and I wouldn't have felt a bit different. For the first time, I saw the world as a hallway with open doors, and I only had to choose which one to walk through. Nothing was closed off for me. I could do anything. Maybe even a marathon.

When we got home, our daughters saw our medals and excitedly asked, "Does this mean you won?"

Without skipping a beat, I confirmed that we had, because we finished.

9

a LITTLE SPARK *of* CORRECTION

The finisher medal from the half marathon became my favorite acces-
sory. It wasn't as pretty as the Park City one, but this one was around
my neck and not some picture on the Internet. I didn't take it off
for hours after the race, and then only because I badly needed a shower.
I wore it to church the next day. It only clashed a little bit with my dress.
People came up to me and asked what on earth I was wearing. I was all
too happy to tell them about it.

"Oh, what's this you ask? I totally forgot I was wearing it. I got it
yesterday by running a half marathon. Yes, that's thirteen point one whole
miles. I just love the number thirteen, don't you?"

Yes, I realize I was terribly obnoxious. I can only ask that you excuse
my behavior as finisher's delirium. The elation from finishing my first
race was a thousand times better that any lame old starter's high. With
finishing, you got to pack two punches: the excitement from starting and
satisfaction of finishing. If I could bottle this feeling and sell it, I would
make millions.

It took a whole week for the giddiness to wear off. I needed more,
but the full marathon was another two months away. I couldn't last that
long, and what if, heaven forbid, I didn't finish that race. After all, it was

like running two half marathons in a row. Would this wonderful feeling disappear and take me from Super Betsy back to Dumpy Betsy? No way, I wouldn't let it. I needed to figure out how to make this feeling last.

It was time for my brain to switch gears again. First I had gone from being a lifelong quitter to making the commitment to never quit. While the no-quitting thing was great and all, it was merely a half measure to keep me from giving up on the things I had to do. It wasn't good enough anymore; now I wanted to be a finisher. A finisher set out to find new challenges on purpose. The non-quitter just kept doing the things that were required. You may not see much of a distinction between the two, but to me they were miles apart—literally. Thirteen point one miles to be exact.

***

Common sense told me that if I wanted to be a finisher, then I needed to look for something to finish. I could go get a bachelor's degree. Naw, going to school was a nice long-term goal, but that wasn't going to help in the immediate future. I could finish that book I'd started, but that would take a long time too. Probably not as long as a four-year degree, but still longer than I wanted to invest right now. I needed something that would take me about a week to complete. I started sifting through the boxes of junk in the guest room, looking for something I'd started that needed to be finished. Around the fourth box, the lightbulb went on in my brain. This room was a disaster. It desperately needed to be cleaned out and organized. I'd known it for a while, but I kept procrastinating because it looked like a lot of work. About a week's worth if I didn't miss my guess.

Sweet! I had purpose again. The next week I ran in the morning and then spent the next few hours on the guest room while the girls were at preschool. Little by little, one box at a time, the room got cleared. I had finished, and looking around the neatly arranged room, I felt that bliss of satisfaction. It wasn't on par with running a half marathon, but then again, I didn't expect it to be. There was also the relief that came from crossing something off the to-do list in my head. Now there was a little more space in the room as well as space in my mind that was previously occupied by nagging reminders of a task needing to be done.

When Jarom got home from work, I covered his eyes to give him the big reveal.

"Ta-da!" I pulled away my hands.

Jarom blinked in either amazement at my fabulous job, or at the sudden influx of light to his eyes.

"Holy cow. Where'd everything go? If I open the closet, will I be hit by an avalanche?" He opened the door cautiously, expecting to be assailed by various camping equipment.

"Nope, just nicely stacked and labeled boxes." Okay, here it came. I was ready for him to tell me what a great wife I was. How he didn't deserve me or, better yet, what he was going to do to prove he deserved me.

The superfluous praise never came. Instead all I got was, "Very nice." And then he walked from the room.

"Very nice? Very nice? I spend a week cleaning, and all you have to say is 'very nice'?" I was incensed, and the timbre of my voice escalated half an octave for each very nice.

"Umm, yeah. Can you do my office next?"

"No, I will not, you little snot. Clean your own darned office." And with that, I stormed out of the room.

I fumed for a good long while muttering to myself. "Why do I even bother? I mean, really! Horribly underappreciated, that's what I am. Well, see if I ever do anything like this again."

Hearing myself whine aloud reminded me why I cleaned the room in the first place, and it wasn't for a pat on the back from Jarom. I was supposed to be basking in the finisher's glow, remember? But thirty years of bad habits are hard to break. It can take a while to retrain your mind into a whole new thought process. And my brain needed a little spark of correction.

Previously I had done things mainly to get accolades and acceptance. I needed to be told what a good job I had done. I wanted to hear that I was special. And before you go thinking that I was a jerk that needed my ego inflated, let me just remind you that I didn't have one. What I was searching for was validation. For someone to tell me I mattered, that my life meant more than the oxygen I used. And that is a hard mind-set to escape.

But I was escaping. I may not have crossed over the wall yet, but I was working on it. I didn't need Jarom to tell me I had done a good job, because I knew I did a good job. The goal of the task was not to be told how wonderful I was; it was to get something done. And I had, therefore, I had finished my goal, and no commentary from the peanut gallery was necessary.

I felt much better, once again finding the peaceful place that finishing something gave me. Now I needed to pick a new task, but still not Jarom's office.

My house was a disaster, so I had plenty of things to choose from. I had kind of settled on cleaning the garage, maybe even digging out all that framing equipment again. There were two impediments to my plan. The first was that my morning runs were taking longer and longer as the mileage increased. It took two and a half hours to run fourteen miles. So my free time before the kids got out of preschool became nonexistent. The other problem was something I hadn't planned on and couldn't have foreseen.

***

In mid-summer, Lily and I went to the dentist and found out that she had seven cavities that needed to be filled. Being a nice mommy, I paid the extra for sedation so she could be more comfortable. Big mistake. She had a "psychotic" reaction to the drugs administered. When she woke up, she was like a wild animal—all claws and teeth. It took an entire day of holding her wrapped in a blanket until she finally calmed down. I figured that was the end of it, and from then on, I'd make sure that we brushed her teeth five times a day so she would never get another cavity.

But that wasn't the end of it. The drugs had trouble leaving her system. That combined with her sensory integration problems gave her major anxiety attacks. Poor kid. She would be fine one second, and then something would startle her like a sound or getting an owie, and boom—flip out. Her nervous system went into overdrive, sending her into a fight-or-flight mode. Understandably, that's scary for a little four-year-old.

Any free time I had was gone, now filled with holding and rocking Lily. Usually she lasted just long enough in preschool for me to finish my run. As soon as I got back, I'd get a phone call telling me to come get her—that she'd had an anxiety attack. I swear that kid is psychic, or has mommy radar, because her timing was impeccable. More often than not I'd have to skip my shower and go get her. The next hour or two was spent calming her and reassuring her that Mommy always came back and no one was going to take her. She followed me around like a little baby duckling; I could rarely be out of her sight. Even bathroom breaks were done in tandem. My other daughter, Autumn, had to spend a big chunk of the day at Grandma's because I couldn't manage both kids. (Thanks, Mom!)

For about a month, every day had its fair share of tears from both Lily and me. Nights weren't much better since she started waking up at all hours from night terrors. Eventually she was afraid to go to bed at all. I had to start getting my runs in before she woke up, which was tricky because she was usually in my bed. It was a rough time for everyone.

Nobody was getting any sleep, so everybody was on edge.

Jarom tried to sympathize with my frustration at not being able to get anything done. He knew I'd had my sights set on cleaning the garage, a rather large undertaking. He would routinely ask me how it was going. One day I snapped.

"How do you think its going? I get maybe five minutes alone at a time. At this rate, I'll never finish anything ever again. I made it an entire day without beating my head against a wall, so I guess I accomplished one thing. Hey, maybe tomorrow I'll see if I can go a whole day without bawling."

"Who said you had to clean the garage? Nobody. I only asked because I knew it was important to you," he snapped back.

"I don't give a crap about the garage. I just want to feel like I've accomplished something. Because holding Lily and not being able to fix it kills me. I can't help her, and I can't help myself. I don't know what to do. I need something good in my day. I think we both do."

Thankfully, Jarom recognized my outburst for what it was: lashing out because at that particular moment on four hours of sleep, life sucked. Instead of further escalating the discussion, he came over and rested his forehead on mine.

"Then find something little you can do together."

It was certainly worth a try. It's not like things could get much worse. So in the mornings, Lily and I would plan out our day, making sure to include a goal that we wanted to do. For the most part, our goals were small and tangible like getting the grocery shopping done. Sometimes we also included intangible goals like trying to get through the day without crying—both of us. On the days that we accomplished our goals, she got a jewel in her treasure chest (our newest reward system). She told me that she loved being "my little helper." That it made her happy.

I truly believe that finishing things together helped Lily. Within a few weeks of being my little helper, her panic attacks became the exception rather than the rule. She wasn't so anxious anymore. I'm sure it was a combination of the doctor, time, and finally sleeping that pulled her through. She had gained the same peace and quiet confidence that I associated with finishing.

Maybe it was just my own feelings rubbing off on her because I felt so much better. I was happy because I learned I could still be a finisher without grand projects every week. I decided I would set a new goal. I would find something to finish every day.

***

Some days I scheduled things that needed to get done. One day, someone at church needed my help fixing her computer. So the goal for that day was to get her computer up and running. It may have taken twice as long as I thought it would plus about five calls to my tech-savvy husband, but I had made a commitment to myself to finish what I started, and I made sure I did just that.

On days that had nothing much going on, I picked something on the to-do list and made sure it got done. Some days were focused on my messy house, like ten loads of laundry needing to be cleaned and folded. And other days all I could manage was focusing on my little ones, like trying not to raise my voice all day. It may not sound like a big deal, but it instituted a change in attitude and lifestyle that I really needed.

Before, I would start the day thinking of all the things that I needed to do and immediately be overwhelmed. Then I'd either run around frantically accomplishing little, or sit on my duff, accomplishing only a deeper imprint in the couch. Nothing much got done, and at the end of the day, I was left with the feeling that the day had been a complete waste.

Now at the end of the day, I knew I could look forward to saying that at least one thing got done. At night, I slept easier knowing I had done the best I could. I no longer felt frazzled and unaccomplished. While I still got a thrill every time I finished something, I had a general feeling of satisfaction that stayed with me. I was a finisher, and I made sure to prove it every day.

That's how I knew that I was going to finish the marathon. All this time I had been going through the motions, doing all the training, saying all the right things, but I never actually believed that I could do it. Not anymore. I was going to prove to myself by running the marathon that anything was possible. If I could go from a 216-pound lump to a lean, mean, marathon-running machine in under a year, then imagine what I could accomplish in five years. Ten?

10

FAT GOGGLES

In the middle of what I've affectionately termed the month from hell, my sister Jaime sent me a present. She's an occupational therapist by trade and deals with children that have much more serious problems than my daughter. If anyone understood my day-to-day struggles with Lily, it was Jaime. For the record, Jaime was the unattributed sister from chapter two that taunted me with Oreos. But we've both grown up in the last fifteen years and have become close friends.

One day, a small box came with a little note, "I know you're having a hard time. It will get better, I promise. I love you." Inside the box was a beautiful silver necklace. It was heart shaped with an Eeyore charm hanging down in the middle. That alone made it an awesome gift. (I'm an aficionado in all things Winnie-the-Pooh.) But what made the gift priceless were the words inscribed on the back: Some days look better upside-down. It's one of my all-time favorite quotes from the gloomy little donkey.

So simple, yet so true. If you don't like the way your day is shaping up, change your point of view. I generally don't recommend standing on your head, though. I tried that in yoga . . . once.

***

Have you ever heard the phrase "hindsight is twenty-twenty"? Well, only if you're wearing the right glasses. If you were wearing beer goggles, rose-colored glasses, sunglasses, or those 3-D glasses, everything you looked at would be different. The glasses that I wore when viewing the past were fat goggles.

That's why I hated pictures. I couldn't look at a picture of me without squinting to see if there's a double chin visible or worse . . . a double lap. One day I was cleaning out my mom's room to help her out. I came across a box of pictures from when I was a kid and a teenager. My first thought was to take the box down and chuck it in the fireplace, but I figured my mom wouldn't appreciate that. Next I wondered where the packing tape was so I could seal this baby up tighter than a time capsule.

Morbid curiosity made me open the box. I figured it would be like looking at the Ghosts of Fat Past again. Thumbing through the pictures made me think that I needed to go get an eye exam. Where were all the pictures of fat me? Had my blessed saint of a mother already gone through and taken them out? I looked closer at the dates on the back. One in particular coincided with my eighth grade year. If I closed my eyes and conjured up an image of what I looked like at thirteen, that picture was not it.

It was a family picture from Hawaii. I remembered the trip vividly. I specifically remembered wearing large oversized tee shirts to swim because I felt so big compared to my smaller siblings and slimmed down parents. Memories portrayed me as a little white whale snorkeling on the beach, but my eyes told a different story now. I hadn't been fat. I wasn't small either, but I wasn't fat. Yes, I was larger than all my sisters, but I was still well within the range of average.

I sat back on the bed, dumbfounded. How was it possible that my memories were so skewed? I spent all my teenage years feeling like the ugly duckling, and this picture was saying that I had been a regular old duck. Thinking back to my youth was a painful process full of feelings of being outcast and inadequate. Starting with the vet's weigh in, I had seen myself as big, and that colored every single experience afterward. My dad had only been trying to help me avoid his pitfalls. Unfortunately in doing so, he made me aware of them in the first place, and I seemed to run headlong for them after I was aware of them. My little obsessive personality would not let it go. I could never see myself as normal or pretty after that. What I saw in the mirror at thirteen was grotesque, but the picture I was looking at now, and I'm sure what other people saw, was just a regular girl that hadn't quite grown out of her baby fat.

The thought that I had needlessly tortured myself for years was almost enough to make me go back on antidepressants again. When you hear something often enough, you start to believe it. When I was teased and taunted as a kid, I began to believe it. Then my little voice started repeating it back to me, distorting my self-image even further. And while I may not have started out very big, I definitely ended up there. But how much is real, and how much is imagined? Even now, some days I struggled to look in the mirror and see that I was any smaller.

I've already established that I was good at lying to myself, and it seemed my mind was good at playing tricks on me too. I realized like with this picture, there were probably plenty of other things I was misremembering. My past was full of battle scars that had never quite healed. But maybe, if I were to go back over them now and see them upside down, so to speak, they would look different.

I gently packed the box back up. I had a lifetime of misconceptions to fix, and it was going to take a whole lot longer than a single afternoon to smooth over. Not now, though. I had a room to finish cleaning. But I had time. My misconceptions weren't going anywhere.

***

After the half marathon, Jarom began having more trouble with injuries. With only two months until the full marathon, we were unsure how he could train without causing more harm to his calf. After reading a book (of course), Jarom decided to try training using the run/walk method. Run/walk is where you run for a specified interval, then walk for a specified interval, then repeat until you've gone the required distance. Jarom's fancy watch even had a special setting built in to accommodate this style of running.

To me it felt like cheating. Would it still count if we ran/walked a marathon? Were there little marathon police that pulled people off the track if they walked? Jarom showed me various articles in running magazines and assured me that it was a popular practice and was even beneficial for preventing injuries and recovering. He programmed his watch to run for four tenths of a mile, and then walk for one tenth. To say that I was skeptical about this new plan, would be putting it mildly.

The run started out normally, and we ran side by side for the first four tenths of a mile. I was just getting in my groove when I heard a *beep, beep, beep* emanating from Jarom's watch. It was time to walk, only I didn't want to—my legs wanted to run. Since I wanted to stick with him and not run ahead, I came up with brilliant idea of running around him while he walked. When the watch beeped again, signaling it was time to run, I went back to running in step beside him. I did that for three miles before I realized that not only did I look like a moron doing some sort of runner's Chinese fire drill, but I was getting tired out from expending way more effort to go the same distance. Plus it annoyed the heck out of Jarom, and he threatened to quit if I didn't knock it off.

So I tried to put my pride aside and walked when the watch beeped. Ugh, I hated it. Seemed like as soon as I'd get comfortable and hit my stride . . . beep. Stupid watch. Recently, I'd been skipping the music and would spend the run conversing with Jarom. This time, I turned up the tunes full blast just to drown out the grumbling in my own head. I was mad at the watch for its incessant squawking yet still unable to resist checking it to sneak a peek at our pace time. What I read did not do anything to endear me further to the device. Here I had worked my butt off to break the ten-minute mile barrier and now those two tenths per mile recovery walking had put me back at eleven-and-a-half-minute miles. I was so grumpy that it made running the remaining seven miles nearly intolerable.

I was having a rough time. It had been easier for me to run the whole thirteen miles of the half marathon than it was to slog through ten miles run/walking. I had never wanted to quit more than I wanted to on that run. It was even worse than the run in the rain. I was in a foul mood when I finally got done and hopped in the shower. I was in foul mood when I picked the kids up from day care. And I was still in a foul mood when I went to bed that night.

I lay there under the covers, stewing about the day's run. Jarom had remarked upon returning home that this had been his easiest run to date. He had enjoyed the change of pace and probably the peace and quiet my cranky silence had given him too. On the other side of the coin, this had been my hardest run. I couldn't make sense of it. Ten miles was ten miles. Why would it be so much tougher today? I wasn't injured physically, but my pride was hurt. And that made my attitude stink. And that was the difference. It felt the same as when I could only run for five minutes at a time, and now somehow I was back to square one. But that wasn't true. I wasn't walking because I was physically unable to run longer; I was run/walking so Jarom could continue to train.

That was my upside-down moment. My brain clicked, and I saw that day's run from a different perspective. Once again I had become obsessed with speed and expectations instead of getting the miles done. What should have been another sticker on my mileage reward chart was instead a huge disappointment. For no good reason—except that I was being a stinker. Just because I learn a lesson once doesn't mean that I don't need refresher courses now and then.

The next run was so much more enjoyable—and easier too. I approached each walk break as an opportunity to rest my knee that was sore from the previous day's run. Our speed was the same if not a little worse than the day before. If we were measuring the success of the run by our pace, then it would have been a failure. Thank goodness we weren't. Jarom and I had a great morning and relished the hour and forty minutes of together time. We finished, and we had fun. So which kind of run did I really want? The faster run by myself with Jarom left by the wayside, or the slower run/walk that was a little harder on me but easier on Jarom? After cardio class that evening, I talked to the Fat Pack about my dilemma. I lamented the loss of my ten-minute mile and explained our new training technique. The pack's speed demon was horrified on my behalf.

"That's awful! What do you think it's going to do to your final marathon time?"

"Well, duh. It's going to slow it down, of course."

"But I think it would be much better to do it together, don't you?" Lori piped in.

I had come to basically the same conclusion but thought I should take a poll to confirm. The tally was two for leaving Jarom in the dust and two for the walk-a-thon. Sarah Michelle was the deciding vote.

"Well, what kind of time are we talking about? How much slower?"

"It will probably take us about forty-five minutes longer doing the run/walk. But I guess that's still faster than if we ran ten-minute miles and couldn't finish."

"Wow, Betsy. That's an awesome way to think about it. Very glass half full."

"Thank you, but I hadn't actually thought about it that way until I said it."

But now that I had said it, that became my new point of view. No matter what time we ended up with, it would be faster than not finishing at all. So if we needed to go a little slower to make sure we could go the distance together, then so be it.

***

Not too long after that, I was talking to a friend at church. She had just run her first half marathon the day before. I noticed that she didn't seem particularly pleased about this fact. She wasn't even wearing her finisher medal.

"So tell me, how did it go?" I chose my words carefully because I wasn't sure if she had finished or not. I didn't want to make her feel bad by asking what it felt like to cross the finish line . . . just in case.

"Oh, it was all right, I guess."

"All right?"

"Yeah, it didn't really go the way I wanted."

Okay, this was like pulling teeth. Rocks would have given me more information. If I wanted to know what happened, I was going to have to come out and ask and hope she wasn't offended.

"So you didn't finish then? Why not?"

"Oh, I finished. My time just stunk."

She'd finished, but she was still upset. Her time must have been really bad, like over four hours bad. Usually you didn't get a medal if you took longer than the allotted time. That must be why she was upset. I was about to give her a heartwarming pep talk when she interrupted my musings with more details.

"I finished in an hour fifty-two. I was really hoping to beat an hour forty-five."

I was flabbergasted. There were so many things wrong with this conversation I didn't even know where to start. My friend had just finished her first half marathon, and instead of being ecstatic, she was upset over seven measly minutes. Then there was the fact that her time was faster than mine by twenty-five minutes, and I didn't care. This was backward. I should be upset that she whipped my butt, and she should be happy to have finished her first race.

"Why on earth did you need to run it in an hour forty-five?"

"That's the time my sister ran her first half in."

"Oh, I see. Well, I guess you can try again next time."

"No way. I'm not doing that again. It wouldn't even count anyway. It had to be on the first one."

I gave her my condolences, and we parted ways, but I was still scratching my head. We had run nearly identical courses, but our experiences were so different. We both finished, and looking at the race data objectively, she had the more successful run. So why was I still secretly wearing my finisher medal at home while she had thrown hers in her closet? Because we had each gone into our respective races with different goals. Mine had been to finish the race with my husband beside me. When I accomplished that goal, I felt on top of the world because I had succeeded. My friend had gone into the race determined to beat her sister's time. So even though she finished the race she still failed in completing her goal. What should have been a proud moment became a disappointment, all because she picked the wrong goal.

That was crazy to me that such a small change in perception would have changed her whole experience. She could have run the exact same race, in the exact same time, but if she had gone into it with the goal of finishing, she would be feeling like a rock star right now rather the loser that couldn't beat her sister.

I had been in real danger of making the same mistake. I so desperately wanted to be able to say that I had run a marathon that I was disappointed I was going to have to admit that I had walked parts. Which is just stupid, because the key part of this was that I would be able to say that I had finished a marathon. It would be the dumbest thing in the world if I done the most impossible thing I could think of and then felt bad because I'd walked. Worse than dumb, it would have been a tragedy. Finishing a marathon was one of the single best moments in my entire life, and I can't imagine having that memory tainted by loser goggles.

11

DON'T THROW *out* YOUR FAT CLOTHES

Opinions are like feet. Almost everybody has them, and sometimes they stink. When I started talking about my marathon goals, everyone seemed to fancy themselves a running expert and had to put their two cents in. Here are a few of the responses I received to my ambitious announcement:

"Really? A marathon? Shouldn't you start a little smaller? I hear they're registering for the toddler trot. You and Lily could enter that."

"I read an article that said running is really bad for your back and knees. In fact, it's probably the worst exercise out there."

"Eleven-minute miles. Well, chin up. I'm sure you can get faster with a little more hard work."

"That's so awesome. A marathon . . . Do you know if the entrance fee is refundable?"

I'm sure people meant well and were just trying to help, but it still hurt. If I was looking for someone to tell me I was crazy to think I could run a marathon, I had no farther to look than myself. I didn't need other people telling me that to reinforce the idea. I was battling my own doubts and worries, so anything other people said ended up just magnifying them.

***

One afternoon, I met a friend for lunch. I had lost sixty-seven pounds at this point and was feeling pleased with myself and how I looked. When I crossed the parking lot and embraced my bud, the first words out of her mouth were these:

"Oh my gosh, you look great! You must be almost done, just another twenty pounds left or so."

My brain did not hear the first part. I skipped the praise and focused on the fact that my friend still thought I needed to lose twenty pounds. That's probably not what she meant, but that's what I heard. Just that morning I had congratulated myself on a job well done. I had reached my goal weight of 150. According to any BMI or height/weight chart, I was now at a healthy weight. Even the clothes from my birthday shopping spree had gotten too roomy, and I'd had to move down to a size 6. I thought a size 6 was small enough, but apparently I was wrong, because my friend still thought I had more to lose. In my head, this equaled saying I was still fat or at least looked that way.

We ordered lunch, and I got the salad instead of the French dip I had been planning on. Her offhanded comment had shaken me, and it was affecting what I ate. What if that's how everyone saw me? What if everyone in this room was thinking the exact same thing, that I was still a little heavy? I obsessed about it until Jarom came home that evening.

"Do I still look fat?" I blurted the minute he walked through the door.

"Hello to you too, dear. My day went well. Thank you for asking."

I went over and kissed him on the cheek. "Hello, how was your day? Do I still look fat?"

My long-suffering eternal companion took off his glasses and scrubbed his hands over his face. "First off, you look amazing, and second, you were never fat. You were just . . . a little . . . Ruebenesque."

It is my firm belief that the best ambassadors must have either chubby or neurotic wives, because being married to me had taught my husband a diplomacy that was not in his natural skill set.

"Then why does Amy think I need to lose weight?"

Jarom threw his hands up in the air. "I don't know. Who's Amy?"

I reminded him who she was and gave him my version of our lunch. I concluded my summary with my concerns that wherever I went, people were secretly guessing my weight and concluding that I was still a little plump.

"Betsy, can I be honest?"

No, lie to me. "Yes." I braced myself to hear the truth, that all my hard work still wasn't enough.

"I don't think people are thinking about you at all. Other than the people who know you, nobody has any idea of what you used to look like. You're just one random person. If anyone notices you, it's because you're looking so cute. But I promise the only person who dwells on your weight is you."

Have I ever mentioned that I love my husband with all my heart? He is my sounding board and the looking glass where only my best features are reflected. When I'm wrong, he'll nudge me in the right direction until I figure it out and then take all the credit. Other than mine, his opinion is the only one that mattered. If he thought I looked amazing, then that was good enough for me. At least for today.

On a side note, the next day I had lunch with my mother. She told me I needed to eat more and that I was looking gaunt. Go figure.

***

I also learned that just because I was letting go of past mistakes didn't mean anyone else was. My well-meaning friends and family have *looong* memories. I had been going through this internal metamorphosis. I felt like a butterfly, but everyone else still saw a caterpillar. My family in particular thought this, and I don't blame them. They have watched many years worth of grand plans that either fizzled out or failed spectacularly. Let's just say they didn't have a whole lot of faith in my newfound stick-to-it-iveness.

One conversation that stands out in my mind was between my dad and me. I love my father, and next to my husband, he's my best friend. So I give his opinion a lot of weight (no pun intended, honestly). I was showing my dad some of the great new outfits I had bought with the birthday money he had given me.

"I love these new clothes, but I'm a little sad about some of the old ones. Like that red wool coat you bought me for Christmas last year. It's my favorite, but it's just too big now. I'm not sure what I should do with them. I don't just want to throw them out. Maybe I should donate them. What do you think?"

"Well, if I were you, I would probably put them in a box and take them out to the garage. If in six months you still haven't gained the weight back, then you can get rid of them."

"So you're saying I should hang on to them?"

"Yes. Don't throw out your fat clothes. It will be difficult and expensive to replace the clothes in the event this is just temporary."

"But I already know that I'm never going to let myself get big again."

"Well, you say that, but so did I, and look how that turned out."

In chapter two, I mentioned that dad had lost 115 pounds when I was twelve. What I didn't say was that by the time I was fourteen he had gained 165 back. Dad absolutely knew what he was talking about. In his mind, he thought he was dispensing practical advice, giving me the benefit of his experience. In my mind, my dad had just told me that he thought I would get fat again. To be fair though, my previous diet history suggested that he was correct.

Like a nervous nelly, I boxed up my fat clothes . . . just in case. I knew in my heart that I had changed. I was a different person now—a happier, healthier, finishing person. But the little voice in the back of my head agreed with my dad—what if.

Flash forward eight months. I was hammering out my little inspirational cubbyholes (if you don't know what I'm talking about, go back and read the introduction) and wanted to nail down the specifics for this chapter. I also wanted to get a little closure on the subject. It's been over a year since I started losing weight, and not a single pound has come back. In fact I've gone ten pounds under my goal weight and have lost seventy-five total. So I went over to my dad's house to see if his opinion had changed.

"So, Dad, it's been a year. Do you still think I might get fat again?"

I had just explained this whole chapter to him and warned that I would be quoting him. I expected profuse apologies at his lack of faith along with promises to never doubt my awesomeness again. So not what I got.

"I don't know, honey. You've done a great job of getting the weight off, but we'll have to wait a few years to know whether or not it will stay off."

It felt like I'd just been hit in the gut. Seriously? It was going to take another two years before my dad believed that I had changed for good. What else did I need to do to show him that was this time was different? *That I was different.* I was smaller than I'd ever been, I'd finished two half marathons and a full, I'd climbed one of the highest mountains in the state, and now I was writing a book about it. I mean really, what was it going to take, because I was fresh out of nearly impossible tasks to finish.

When we'd had this conversation last time, I had walked away hurt and resentful about his lack of support. I had taken the nonconfrontational approach and kept my pain to myself, letting it fester. It had stayed sore for a while. I knew better now and had the confidence to say something about it.

"I know you didn't intend it to, but that really hurts my feelings."

"I was just being honest with you."

"Yes, and I appreciate that, but what I just heard was that you don't think I can do it. That I can stay small. You think I'm going to fail."

"But that's not what I meant."

"I figured as much, and that's why I'm telling you so that you can understand the way that makes me feel."

"But I was just thinking that statistically speaking, the odds are against you. More often than not people gain weight back. I did. It really wasn't about your ability to keep it off."

His left-brained logical approach combined with personal experience had colored his perception, making it difficult to separate my experience from his. But I'm not him, and I'm not a statistic. I'm me, and my experience is unique. Different than any other, even my own past attempts. I know I won't ever go back to those XXL pants again. If it takes dad five years to get the memo, that's okay.

I left the house lighter, happy that we had cleared up the miscommunication. He hadn't intended to hurt my feelings; we just looked at things differently. If I chose to be offended, then it was my own fault, because there was no malice in his words.

***

Ninety percent of the time, people meant well and didn't mean to be rude. After I realized that they often had no clue what they were talking about, I stopped being hurt. But then there's the other 10 percent. For whatever reason, these people walk around with a chip on their shoulder and get their satisfaction from watching other people feel bad. Thankfully none of my family is like that; however, I did run, literally, into some people that were. I have no idea who they were, so I just started calling them Hell's Speedwalkers, otherwise known as the gang of six old ladies that take up the whole stupid track.

After completing his dream of finishing a marathon, Jarom decided to hang up his running shoes. I, on the other hand, had actually come to enjoy running. I know, who'd have ever thought? Certainly not me. I had learned to appreciate the peace and quiet a leisurely three-miler gave me when I wasn't concerned about time or training for something. Three times a week, I went to the park and ran. It was on one of those mornings that I met those evil octogenarians.

On my second lap around the track, I saw them. They were walking six ladies wide across the whole track, going counterclockwise. I was running clockwise and assumed common courtesy would take over and they would either split down the middle or one of them would move ahead or behind and make a hole. I watched and waited to "thread the needle" as it's referred to in runners' circles, but as I drew closer, they just glared at me with steely eyes and did not budge.

So in our game of chicken, I flinched first or, more accurately, I ran off the course, tripped over the edge, and landed face-first in the grass. Those witches actually cackled and kept right on speed walking. I was mortified, and all those feelings of inadequacy came rushing back. I went home defeated, letting myself end a run early with no injuries for the first time since the no-quit pledge.

At first I was embarrassed. I felt like I was back in high school, when the mean kids would trip me and play pranks at my expense. I would probably have to change my run times since I was afraid that I would run into them again. Or maybe just switch to a different park. Those kind of thoughts lasted until I got out of the shower, and by then, my fear had turned to fury. Who the heck were these old bags that they had the power to make me feel like a loser? I was not a loser. I had run a marathon for goodness sake. Well run, walked, and limped one, but I'm getting ahead of myself. The point was, nobody could make me feel like a failure but me.

There was no way I was going to let those hags chase me off. I was there first, and I was not changing my run for the likes of them. So two days later, I went back and sure enough they were there, but this time I was prepared. No, I didn't bring water balloons to chuck at them, though that would have been fun. When they didn't move, I ran around them, watching my step a little more carefully this time.

They heckled and whispered and laughed. I briefly considered telling them off, but that wouldn't have solved anything and probably would have created a bigger problem. (Old ladies are vicious.) Instead, I opted to be the bigger person so I smiled, said good day, then blazed past them. We repeated this play ten times or more on the three-mile run.

The next Friday, it was the exact same thing. I considered amending my racing animal analogy to include these nuisances. Maybe they could be the slugs? Or better yet, territorial elephant seals in ugly tracksuits displaying their dominance. You know it's not paranoia if people are really out to get you, and these ladies did not like me there. I'm hoping they hated runners in general and not just me. Perhaps they had pace envy and felt bad that they were so slow. For whatever reason, they chose to antagonize me. We faced off three days a week for a month. They never budged, and I never quit. At the end of the month, the weather turned colder, and one day they stopped coming, but I didn't. Now the frost and I have the track to ourselves. The penguin wins again.

***

I can't control what other people do or say. It's just not within my sphere of influence. The only thing I can do is put my best effort out there and be confident in the knowledge that I've done everything I could. Someone is going to try to rain on my parade. It's inevitable, and there's not a darn thing I can do to stop them. What I can do is decide how I'm going to respond. As a rule, I try to give as much thought to the comment as the person did in making it. After all, why should I spend weeks crying over what somebody said off the top of his or her head?

Throughout this year, I had to learn to deal with not only my own little voice but also all the other nuts from the peanut gallery. Locking myself in my room or using earplugs wasn't really an option. While there is something to be said for being a hermit, avoidance was no longer my answer.

12

DOES GOD HAVE *a* RETURN POLICY?

gnoring what other people said soon became second nature. What I was still having issues with, however, were the things I said to myself. Or it might be more accurate to say the problem lay in the way I saw myself. The little voice in my head was so quiet now that I could hardly hear it. I no longer berated myself about quitting or my accomplishments. I proudly stood by all the things I was finishing. This problem was deeper and much more sinister. While I had learned to take credit for the things I had done, I still wasn't happy with who I was. When I looked in the mirror, I saw someone who was different, flawed . . . broken.

I was born with severely crossed eyes, a condition known as strabismus. I got my first pair of coke-bottle glasses at six weeks old. Two years and eight surgeries later, the doctors managed to sever and reconnect the muscles in my eyes, allowing them to appear mostly straight. Unfortunately there wasn't much they could do for the vision itself. My eyes were unable to focus at the same time on the same object, resulting in being classified as legally blind. Only one eye was able to see at a time, meaning I had almost no depth perception. I'm pretty sure people used to think my mom beat me as a kid because I was covered head to toe in bruises from walking into things. When I got a black eye and the school nurse asked where it came from, she didn't believe I had actually run into the doorknob.

The doctors kept tinkering on my eyes with more surgeries and eye patches. In first grade, the kids ran away from me because they thought I was a pirate. Now if I were cool, I would have pretended to have a peg leg too and chased after them saying "Arrr." Instead I kept mostly to myself and stayed in with the teacher at recess. When I wasn't wearing a patch, the eye I wasn't actively using would wander off.

Kids, being kids, saw my weakness and attacked. They were the lions, and I was a nice juicy zebra. The children fit into two categories: ones that were honestly confused about where I was looking and the kids that were just plain mean. The former (and adults still do this surreptitiously) would glance around, trying to figure out what I was looking at. The latter would find some excuse to come talk to me but then make a specific point to stare off into space for the entire conversation. Then they ran back to their friends and laughed.

When confronted with adversity and bullying, a person can toughen up and develop a thick skin. Not me, I got thicker, but my skin was paper-thin. Each harsh word and joke at my expense cut deeply and I felt it down to my soul. In sixth grade my parents thought I might have asthma, but it turned out I was just hyperventilating from panic attacks at school. That's the same time I realized I was a little bit bigger and sturdier than most kids. I was different; something about me was wrong.

I became obsessed with fitting in, being normal . . . finding perfection. If I could be the perfect ideal, then everyone would love me and the children wouldn't tease me anymore. I wanted to look like Barbie, and no matter what I tried, I didn't. The confluence of factors mentioned above created one chubby, depressed teenager. I learned quickly to put on a façade for my parents and teachers. The last thing I needed was to end up in the nuthouse.

But that was all fake, and I knew it. At school, I would play the part of the clown and laugh with the rest of kids when someone put dog food in my locker. At home I spent hours on my knees, praying for God to fix whatever was wrong with me that everyone hated so much. When that didn't help, I prayed to go to sleep and not wake up.

Obviously, the Lord opted not to recall my serial number, so I decided that he needed a little assistance. Without any planning or premeditation, I woke up one morning and swallowed two weeks' worth of pills that my parents' doctor had given me to assist with weight loss. This is why I said giving a depressed teenager a bunch of pills was a very bad idea. Luckily for me, the roughly one hundred pills were mostly vitamins, calcium, and a mild appetite suppressant. If they had included the fen-phen and thyroid medications that my parents were taking, I would have been toast. Would have made the worst obituary ever . . . death by diet pills.

Obviously I didn't die, but boy I sure felt bad enough that I wished I had. The mask of happiness that I had so carefully constructed fractured, allowing everyone to see just how messed up I really was. My parents tried to get me help and every quack had a theory on what was wrong with me. Juvenile schizophrenia? Nope. Manic depression. Still a no. In the meantime, they pumped me so full of drugs that I couldn't feel a single thing. With a cold indifference I saw my nervous breakdown as further evidence of just how far from everyone else I really was.

Finally, when I was sixteen, my newest doctor settled on a diagnosis of post-traumatic stress disorder. What was so traumatic? Life, I guess. I felt too much, but that was better than the hollow nothingness the over-prescribed lithium gave me. The doctor immediately took me off all the heavy-duty stuff and found a nice balance with Zoloft. It didn't fix me, but it made my emotions easier to deal with. But the medication couldn't stop me from comparing myself to everyone else and knowing that I didn't measure up.

The next fifteen years were filled with highs and lows in weight and emotions. I wanted to be someone else, anyone else. Someone that didn't need to take medication, someone that didn't have weight problems, somebody that had two working eyes, and the list went on and on. Recently, when the doctor took me off the antidepressants for the first time since adolescence, I felt like I was one step closer to fitting in—to assimilating with all the regular people (horrible attitude, I know). I would no longer feel the secret shame I associated with taking the pills.

Initially, when the extra pounds started coming off, I was ecstatic. Soon I would look just like everybody else. But before long, the newness of my smaller body wore off and I began to look at my new shape more critically. I'd lost seventy or so pounds and now weighed around 145 pounds. That still sounded like a lot. My sister in-law was just a little shorter than me and she was under 120 pounds. Aside from the number itself, I didn't look like I thought I would. I was hoping to have a smooth hard body with a flat tummy and perky breasts. Instead I still had stretch marks all over and loose, saggy skin. And while I had gone from a size 16/18 to a 4/6, my top half had also dropped from a double D to a middle B.

When I went to the gym, I couldn't help but notice that I still didn't look like all the cute petite girls in Zumba class. They were bigger on top, smaller in the middle, and appeared generally more delicate. As for me, I was still nowhere close to delicate. I could look at myself for ages in the mirror after my shower, pointing out all my flaws. While I could now see all my ribs, the rib cage itself was much wider and broader than the other girls I wanted to be like. In particular, I wanted to look like my husband's two little sisters. They were slight, where I was thick. After a family dinner, I lamented this fact to Jarom.

"It's not fair. Why don't I look like your sister?" I said while undressing.

"Well, for starters, I'm really glad you don't look like my sisters."

I thumped him with the pillow. "You know what I mean. I'm frustrated because even though I'm working my butt off, I don't think I can ever be that little. I'm pretty sure that if you took our skeletons and laid them out, side by side, I still wouldn't look like her. I'd still be bigger."

"You're probably right. That's the way genetics works."

"Well, that sucks. Fix it."

"I can't. It's just the way you were built."

"Then I was built wrong."

"Says who?"

"Says me. It's all wrong. I'm all wrong."

Saying it out loud took more than I had to give at that moment, and I broke down into quiet sobs. My tank was on empty, emotionally, physically, and spiritually. I was giving everything I had to keep my family afloat, train for the marathon, keep the weight off, and resist the lure of the pie in the fridge. I had changed so much and worked so hard and the thought that all my efforts would never be enough to take me where I thought I needed to be tore me open.

My husband waited patiently for me to get myself under control. Or enough that I could form a cohesive sentence. "My bones are too thick, my eyes don't look straight, and I'm an emotional wreck. I'm just exhausted."

And I was—tired, that is. I hadn't been sleeping because of all the things with my daughter. I also knew that I wasn't taking in near the amount of calories my body needed to repair itself after the two- to three-hour runs in the mornings. Yep, I was both tired and terrified that if I ate what I needed to I would get fat. Terrified too that if I had to take antidepressants again I would prove once and for all that I was deficient, that I needed an outside source to become whole. I blubbered something to that effect to my husband. Instead of gathering me into his arms as I had come to expect, he got mad. It's pretty rare for Jarom to get angry, but when he does, watch out.

"So what you're saying is that because I have to take medication for diabetes, I'm defective."

"No, I'm not talking about you. It's not your fault that your pancreas decided to stop with the insulin. Don't be stupid."

"And it's your fault that something in your brain stopped making serotonin?"

"Well, no, but I could probably deal with it better."

"What? Just buck up and be happy? So if you can't control your emotions perfectly, you're not as good? You're not allowed to be afraid or cry or have a tough time?" Jarom kept getting louder, almost to the point where I was concerned he would wake the kids.

"It means I'm broken. Because normal people don't have these problems."

Jarom stopped fuming and became still and quiet, a bad sign. "So does that mean that you think Lily is broken? That we should ask God to take her back? Do you love her any less because she isn't the perfect, happy girl you want her to be?"

The only sound in the room was my sharp intake of breath. It was a good one too, because I don't think I breathed again for a few minutes. Jarom had said the most awful thing I had ever heard in my life. I was offended that he would even think such a horrible thing. How could he possibly think that I would change my baby to anything else or think she was less? Probably because that was exactly how I felt about me, and he was afraid I would judge her by my own harsh standards. I'd never held the measuring stick of normalcy up to anyone else; I was too busy judging myself to judge anyone else. What if I had somehow unintentionally given Lily that impression, though, that she wasn't enough?

Previously, I had stopped crying so that I could argue with Jarom, but now I began with a new intensity. My heart broke at the mere thought that I might have made my little one feel anything less than treasured for exactly who she was.

"No. She's Lily, and she's perfect just the way she is," I stammered out in between gasps for air.

Not that he would ever admit it, but Jarom's eyes held a little bit of shine from water overflow too. "I know, and you are too. You're Betsy, and you're perfect just the way you are."

We didn't say anything else, just snuggled and went to bed. Well,

Jarom went to bed. I couldn't sleep because my brain was busy processing. The angry insinuation that I might devalue Lily because of her situation was like a slap to the face. It also did more for me than the one hundred pep talks he'd given me in the past. I couldn't look at myself as a mistake anymore, not without implying that Lily wasn't good enough too. It wasn't like hitting a switch and saying "Aha! You're cured!" But it did get the gears in my mind spinning, thinking about what exactly I had been trying to fix all this time.

***

Over the next week or so, I began looking at everyone with the same lens that I looked at myself with. Those perfect girls at the gym, they only accounted for maybe 10 percent of the population. And just between you and me, I'm pretty sure those teeny-waisted, well-endowed women might have had a little work done. Not that there is anything wrong with having plastic surgery. I'm just saying that it would be nice if they wore a shirt or something alerting me to that fact. You know like, "Yes, I know I'm gorgeous, and it was worth every penny." That way, I wouldn't feel the pressure to live up to an unnaturally high standard.

For every one of them, there were nine other women all wonderfully flawed and unique. Why hadn't I seen them before? It's like I had blinders on that only let me see the women that I thought were better and prettier, and I lost the rest in background. I'm not sure if you have ever noticed, but background takes up most of the picture. And the picture of what a woman is would be composed mostly of the women I had previously dismissed as inconsequential.

The ladies in my Fat Pack are powerful, beautiful, and amazing women. And every single one of them moaned and groaned about something they don't like about themselves. My tummy is too big; my arms are too short; my knees are too knobby. One of the other trainers, Star, played college rugby and was super buff. She was toned and looked awesome. If there was anything that I thought I could ever come close to realistically achieving, she was it. We were similar height and body types and we tended to pack muscle on easily (fat too if we're not careful). Star's self-observed weakness was that her thighs and calves were too large for her taste, even though they were solid muscle. She also wanted to be teeny, tiny, and delicate. I was floored. She looked great and still she wanted to be someone else too. Where was my ideal? What was the perfection I had been reaching for? I had been killing myself working out seven hours a week in addition to my running, just trying to be the right size and shape. Well, who the heck gets to determine what "right" is?

I was now thoroughly confused. Was everyone broken? Was that just the nature of the human condition? That didn't seem right, and if it was, then I didn't want to live that way anymore. I found the answer with a knee in the back. At yoga one night, I was doing the stretch where you are sitting on the ground and you reach out toward your toes. The correct way to do this is to keep your back straight and reach out, stretching from your hips. Well, that got me to about my knees, and that would not do. I wanted to touch my toes, because . . . I have no idea. Probably because I thought it was something everybody should be able to do, and therefore I wanted to be as good as everyone else. So I curled my back into the shape of a C and reached until my fingers brushed my big toe, which was as bent back as far as it would go (I needed the extra inch). Abruptly, a knee pushed into my lower back and strong hands brought my shoulders back into line.

"No, more like this," the instructor gently (at least vocally) corrected. She continued on as she returned to the front of the room. "You don't get any better stretch in the hips if your back is doing the reaching. You don't have to be able to touch your toes. Do what you can. Wherever you are is the right place to be."

That last part really stuck with me as I pondered it more after class. I put so much effort into trying to be as good as everyone else that I was always trying to fix myself. What if I was never broken to start with? What if I was just a work in progress? A masterpiece at any stage is still a masterpiece. Instead of trying to imitate someone else's work of art, I would be my own. If at any point (and there are still plenty) I'm unhappy with the way things are shaping up, then I need to realize that wherever I am is still a good place to be. I will change and evolve from one day to the next, because time never stands still. Tomorrow I will be something else, and that will be good too.

It is my sincerest hope that by learning to accept myself as I am, I can teach my daughters the same lesson. That they will grow up to be happy and confident women who know that I will always love them because of their flaws, rather than in spite of them.

I'm loud, quirky, and a little bit neurotic. I will never be one of the world's great beauties. But that's how I was made. I'm exactly what I was designed to be. And since I have a husband, kids, family, and friends that love me, those things must not be too bad. My differences make me unique, a limited edition.

13

BURNING *the* BLUE FLORAL PARACHUTE

My garage was home to Pandora's box, otherwise known as my fat clothes. The Rubbermaid containers only took up a small corner, but every time I passed them, they seemed to grow larger. Was it possible for my fat clothes to get fat without me? I began to hate going into the garage, because I knew those boxes would be waiting for me. They were the physical representation of my own doubts and fears. I mentally beat myself up, Why are they still there? Why can't I just toss them out? Because they were an insurance policy. I could dress it up as being smart and practical like my dad had suggested, but that was a lie.

Those boxes reminded me every time I saw them that I was afraid I would need them again someday. It's kind of ironic, actually. I used to keep a big gray box of size 10 clothes that had fit briefly during one of my diet successes. That gray box represented a hope that I would one day be that skinny again. Soon after sealing them up, I gave the clothing to my sister because she could use them, and I resigned myself to the fact that I would never fit them.

So why had I been so quick to toss out hope but slow to give up doubt? I rationalized that it was just a backup plan, a safety net. But why did I need a safety net? Probably because I had fallen so often that I felt I needed one. There was a war going on in my mind. Part of me said that if I was truly committed to keeping the weight off, I would throw those clothes out. Yet there they were, taking up precious space in my garage and thoughts. That said to me that even I wasn't sure I could keep the weight off. And that stung.

I decided that I needed to do the unthinkable and open Pandora's box, just to see what I was so desperately clinging on to. First thing I saw under the lid was a bright-blue tent. I had to recheck the label on the box to make sure it said Old Clothes and not Camping Gear. I shook out the fabric to get a better look. It was not a tent but rather an XXL blue floral muumuu from last summer's trip to Hawaii. Somebody must have spiked my non-alcoholic piña colada, because my judgment had to have been seriously impaired to buy that. So what was my excuse for saving it?

Sifting through the rest of the box, I found not only more clothes, obviously, but also the memories attached to each piece. The red coat my dad had given me for Christmas. The Winnie the Pooh overalls that made me smile whenever I wore them. The dress I wore on my tenth wedding anniversary dinner.

Opening the box had also opened my eyes to a few things. For one, I had a horrible fashion sense. And for another, a part of me found comfort in my fat clothes. I had spent most of my life overweight; it was familiar territory. But this new me was different and scary, and I didn't know what to expect. It's like I was flying high and these clothes were my parachute (the muumuu could probably be used as one). It was the assurance that I could float back to my comfortable old life at anytime.

I needed to make a choice: Did I want my safe old life back as a lump on the sofa or did I want a new life of reaching higher with the risk of falling? I had made a decision and wanted to share it with the Fat Pack, so I donned the muumuu one last time and wore it to cardio class (over my workout clothes). Muumuus aren't that flattering when they fit properly, but when they're four sizes too big, it's a crime against nature. Sharon was horrified that such a thing even existed. Sarah Michelle and Lori were impressed that you could fit two of me in the dress now. And Mallory wanted to take it home with her.

I agreed with the first two opinions and decided for the third that I liked Mallory too much to burden her with my fashion faux pas. Friends don't let friends wear muumuus. Talking to my girls had given me the support and courage I needed to let go. They believed in me, Jarom believed in me, and I was pretty sure I could believe in me too.

***

The big blue muumuu wasn't the only parachute I had lying around. Turned out I also had a steady supply of fire escapes and trapdoors as well. While using the run/walk method had helped Jarom's calf, as the mileage increased, it still bothered him too much to run more than once a week. That left me to run three out of four runs by myself. Running fourteen miles with Jarom had been a morning activity, difficult but doable. Running fourteen miles by myself was a morning chore, arduous and exponentially tougher.

Jarom and I had started our running career doing laps around the park track, but have you ever gone in circles for ten miles? Gets boring real fast. So we decided that anything over eight or so miles, we would leave the park and see what little back roads we could discover together. It had been fun seeing where our feet would take us and using Jarom's watch to figure our way back. One time we overshot and ended finishing the day's run a mile from home. But most of the time Jarom's uncanny sense of direction and distance would get us back right on time.

When God was handing out that particular skill I must have been in the buffet line, because I get lost on my way to the bathroom . . . in my own house. What on earth was I supposed to do without him next to me, telling me where to go? My confident morning runs had abruptly become scary to me. What if I got lost or had to go to the bathroom or hurt something and needed help? It wasn't even too big a stretch. I routinely tripped over uneven sidewalks and curbs because of my vision, and Jarom had always been there to pick me up and dust me off. The night before my first big solo run, I had nightmares about falling in a ditch, twisting an ankle, and lying there alone and helpless until Jarom missed me and sent out a search party.

I decided that I should make small circles around the house . . . just to be safe. Then I would be close enough to home if I found myself unable to complete the run. Each time I passed the house, my little voice whispered that I could go inside and be done for the day. It was too hard, and I was alone. The temptation, added to the uneasiness of being by myself, made the training much more difficult than it should have been.

I began to seriously doubt my ability to run a marathon. It seemed too hard, and I was still ten miles shy with sixteen miles being the longest distance I had gone. What if Jarom's leg didn't get better? Did I still want to do it if I had to by myself? It was looking increasingly more like that might be the case. Jarom and I had been waffling back and forth on the wisdom of getting a hotel next to the start line or driving the hour or so from home the morning of the race. Good thing I had procrastinated getting a hotel room in Park City. After all, those things were nonrefundable.

Hello, escape hatch. Without even meaning to, I hadn't fully committed myself to my goal. I still had a foot on the fire escape. How on earth did I expect to make it all the way through twenty-six point two grueling miles when I wasn't even sure if it was worth it to rent a room? I was spending way too much energy worrying about what to do if I failed when I should have been spending all those resources on making sure I didn't,

It was high time to start closing the back doors. First, I remedied the hotel situation and booked a room at the Best Western (just in time too; they were almost sold out). I still wasn't sure if Jarom was running or not, but I was going to plan as if we were. Next was changing my running route, no more little circles for me. I was going to run far and wide and enjoy seeing new sights again. Another thing that helped me was a little positive peer pressure, as in I told everyone and their dog that I was running a marathon. Church leaders: check. Extended family: check. Cashier at grocery store: check.

My mother was convinced that I was setting myself up to fail, but it was just the opposite. I was setting myself up for success and planning as if success was inevitable. The more action and positive pressure I applied, the better I felt about the marathon. It was easier to visualize completing it the more I talked about doing it.

***

Running wasn't the only thing I needed to plan for. Getting rid of my fat clothes would be pointless without a solid plan to make sure it stayed off. Call it fire prevention if you want. And that's how I discovered the Goldilocks principle.

I've always been a little (a lot) obsessive, "all or nothingish" in my personality. So it's no surprise that I had become obsessed with the scale. The enemy I used to avoid was now a reference I checked every day to make sure I had not been eating cheesecake in my sleep or something. In the height of my obsession, it was not uncommon to weigh myself five times in a single day. Just in case someone slipped lard into my water or something. Addictions rarely pass the common sense test. Point is I was going way overboard trying to make sure I didn't gain a single pound back.

I was even hesitant to use energy gels (fast carbs for energy in the middle of a run) because that was one hundred calories less I could count as burning off from a long run. After hitting the wall a few times, I quickly realized that the energy gained was worth the price of calories spent.

There were days that I would go to sleep at night with my tummy growling and my body so sore from an overabundance of exercise and think, "Surely this cannot be good for me." My yoga instructor thought so as well. One evening she asked me what the tattoo on my shoulder blade meant (misspent youth—don't ask). I told her it was the Japanese Kanji character meaning "balance." She got a wry smile and bit the inside of her cheek to keep from laughing. At first I thought it was from irony considering I had just fallen on my bum trying to do chair pose. But she assured me that is was more to do with the fact that I was always coming in to class frantic, stressed, and sore from doing too much. What I needed was more balance, both in class so I didn't tip over, and in my life in general.

For some unknown reason, the story of Goldilocks came to mind. That girl was always trying everything. This porridge was too hot, that one was too cold. But what was the last one . . . just right. I needed to stop doing too much and eating too little and find my just right. And that's why I call it the Goldilocks principle: finding a balance and moderation in the things I was doing so my porridge would be "just right."

My daily weigh-ins with my frenemy, the scale, had to go. Instead of letting fear get the best of me, I needed to look at the situation rationally. How had I lost the weight in the first place? By eating less and moving more. I had found a caloric balance with my body, as long as I burned more calories than I took in, I lost weight. It was like any other budget. If I spent more calories than I'd burned then I would inflate just like the national debt. We didn't want that. By the same logic, if I didn't spend enough calories, then I couldn't cover what I was expending. I might get skinnier, but my body's energy would be rock bottom.

If I wanted to eliminate both the daily weight fluctuation freak-outs and the energy crashes, then I needed to balance the budget. So I made a plan, and I figured out exactly how many calories I was burning a day and made sure I ate very close to that same amount. I wasn't trying to lose another pound; I just wanted to maintain and feel good. I was amazed at all the things I needed to eat just to make up for calories burnt on a fourteen-mile run. That's fifteen hundred calories, two giant ooey gooey cinnamon rolls. And let me just tell you how much easier it is to get through a long run when you know that you not only have the energy reserves but you've also earned the baked good waiting at home for the refuel. (A cinnamon roll tastes better too when you've earned it.)

It actually worked. I was no longer completely exhausted by the end of the day, and my tummy stopped grumbling too. And I didn't gain a single pound. As long as I carefully plotted and stayed within my budget, I was fine. I started to trust the facts and stop worrying that I would gain another mysterious ten pounds overnight again. Because after all they weren't too mysterious, were they? I had just blinded myself to how much I was eating. For the first time in a year, I went on a camping trip without having to bring the scale with me to check on my progress.

***

It would probably be unreasonable to expect that I will always be within one pound of my lowest number. In fact, I'm pretty sure all of those holidays like Valentine's Day, Easter, Halloween, Thanksgiving and Christmas are all heavily promoted by the candy and weight loss companies. They're are out to get me, I swear. It's like supply and demand: supply me the candy, and then I'll have to demand the weight loss. But I've got a plan for that too. I now weigh myself once every two weeks, because if at any time I reach 150, eight pounds more than I am now, then I'll know that I need to reevaluate the budget. Why the arbitrary eight pounds? Supposedly ten to twelve pounds equal one dress size, and I am not about to go and buy bigger clothes. So I planned a fail-safe to make sure I don't have to. At the eight-pound mark, I redo the math and start moving more and eating less all over again. It's a whole lot easier to lose eight pounds than seventy-five.

But what if it's a holiday five pounds? Then I'm not going to worry about it. Why not? Well, for one, because I'm happy with where I'm at now, and five pounds is not going to change that. For another, I know I have a sound plan to ensure my success, and for me that means no longer spending countless hours worrying over what could go wrong. I have a commitment to succeed, and if something should dare get in my way, then I will make a new plan and another and another until I get it right.

Let me tell you what happened to Pandora's box. I opened it and found all the evils (the muumuu) but also found hope (my memories). So some clothes I donated, but others had a different destination. Currently on my to-do list, after completing this book, is to make a quilt. A fat quilt. Yep, with the squares made from pieces of my favorite fat clothes.

My anniversary dress, the embroidered Pooh bear from my overalls, and more. They can keep me warm at night with their happy memories, without being a safety net. Because I know I don't need one anymore, but I do need to keep warm because I get a lot colder in winter without the extra built-in insulation.

As for the blue muumuu and a few other choice pieces with some not so good memories attached—I burned them. Some things are too ugly even for a patchwork quilt. But seriously the experience was cathartic and once again cheaper than therapy. I was burning my safety line and effectively killing any last whispers from my little voice saying I thought I might get fat again. There were no prayers offered for the crematory of my things, but I think the weight-loss gods approved of my sacrificial offering. The fire burned with intensity and unnatural hues, so I was either getting a big thumbs-up, or it was a sign that polyester and rayon should not be burned. Either way, the blue, green, and orange flames were beautiful to watch.

14

the FIGURATIVE THUD and LITERAL CRASH—AGAIN

had been taking yoga now for months so I could get my body more flexible. Too bad it did nothing for my flexibility when moving around life's little obstacles. I was still rigid in my determination and in my goals. I had a vision of what my marathon would look like and nothing was going to alter that because I was in control of my life. Right? Well, even though I was the driver on the road of life, that didn't mean there weren't potholes and flat tires.

Three weeks before the marathon, things were looking up. Jarom and I finished our final long run of the training program, eighteen miles equaling three hours and forty minutes. It was my favorite run of all time. My legs felt great, I had the right amount of energy, and at the end I still felt like I could squeak out the other eight miles to complete the required twenty-six point two. I was ready, and I knew with an absolute certainty that I was going to finish a marathon. Jarom was still a little iffy and had not felt at ease with the distance, let alone doing eight more. I told him that I'd drag him across if I had to.

We both breathed a sigh of relief at completing the high mileage portion of the training. For the next three weeks instead of getting bigger, the runs would get smaller, allowing our legs to heal from any small strains and micro-tears. It's called tapering. According to running experts, running eighteen miles is no different than running the whole twenty-six, at least as far as your endurance and body are concerned (yeah, try telling that to my legs after the extra hour and a half). The point was that you risked injury by stressing out your body with any more high-mileage runs before the race. I was cool with that; I could use a break.

I really should know better than to tempt fate. It's like saying, "What else can go wrong?" or "I sure hope it doesn't rain." About a week after the long run, I ran the absolute fastest I have ever run in my life . . . to feed the parking meter. We were at a local university, registering Jarom for classes. I must be a good influence on my husband, because he decided to be a finisher too and go back to college and get his degree. The visitors parking is meter based, and our time had run out while we were waiting to meet his advisor; so it was my job to run to the car, toss a few quarters in, and get back before they called Jarom's name. (He needed the moral support.)

You'd think I would be smarter than to run full speed without stretching, but no. I opened up my inner throttle and let loose, pleased to be running fast for once and not at Jarom speed. Pride will bite you in the butt every time. We were in a hurry because after the meeting we were all headed out to Yellowstone on a camping trip to celebrate Jarom's birthday. I wasn't thinking. Running fast would be do-over number one.

There was no sharp pain or any indication of injury while I was running. I had no clue anything was wrong until about two hours into the drive to the national park. That would be re-do number two, to not stay in an uncomfortable seated position, inflaming the injury more. When we stopped at a rest area, I knew something was off. I hopped out of the car and my eyes flew open from the sudden influx of pain. My left leg collapsed underneath me. I could not physically make it to the restroom without Jarom's help. At this point I had no clue what was wrong. I was putting my money on my leg being asleep or some blood circulation thing. Since I hadn't felt any trauma at the time, it didn't occur to me that I had injured it sprinting.

After the potty break, I walked around for a minute, and that seemed to work out most of the pain. Now it was just sore and uncomfortable but manageable. I chalked it up to sore muscles frozen up from the drive. When we got the RV parked, I would be sure to stretch out. That night, I iced my leg with the frozen corn we'd brought. The next morning was my long run, but it was only nine miles. (How crazy that I was thinking only nine miles?) Jarom had decided that his version of tapering meant no running at all for three weeks, so I was going to be on my own. If my leg was still sore in the morning, then I would swap runs with the short in two days and do four miles instead, just to be safe.

Four miles was still a wee bit optimistic. After exiting the RV, I made it down the trail maybe one hundred yards before my eyes were tearing up in pain. Perhaps if I walked a slow lap around the campground, my leg muscles would warm up and I could try a slow jog. Step and wince, step and wince. I would not give up, so I tried running again. Exactly eight steps later I had to stop or drop. This couldn't be happening to me. For the first time since beginning of my adventure, I quit a run early. I hobbled back to the RV in tears from the wrenching pain in both my hamstring and my heart.

I had slipped out that morning without waking Jarom or the kids, but when I tripped over the stairs attempting to get into the RV, the thud woke everybody. Why is it that the low points in my life all have the figurative thud and the literal crash? Just an observation. Anyway, this time I was not naked when he gathered me up off the floor, but my soul was laid bare. Even though I was afraid to give voice to me fears, something was seriously wrong with my leg. The girls woke up and cried with me. They had no idea what was going on; they just knew Mommy had an owie and was crying. I calmed myself down so the girls would calm down too and so our next campsite neighbors wouldn't wake up from my children's siren-like wails.

Jarom made pancakes, and we all sat down, ate, and discussed what the heck was going on. I finally put my finger on the culprit, a pulled hamstring, most likely from the parking meter sprint. Next, I quizzed my nearest source of information, Jarom. Surely he had read some book on the subject, so maybe he could play doctor and diagnose and fix it. He had, of course, read a sports injury book and examined my leg and asked a hundred questions. Is there bruising? Does it burn? Is there a stabbing pain or more of a rending pain? In the end he gave his non-expert opinion, which was later confirmed by the sports people. I most likely had a second-degree strain of the hamstring.

Well, super. How long would that take to fix? The answer was four to eight weeks, depending on the severity. I didn't have four weeks! The marathon was in sixteen days. For probably the first time ever, I hoped that Jarom was stupid and had no idea what he was talking about. I was mourning the loss of my dream, and the first stage is denial. Maybe if I pretended that it wasn't really hurt, the pain would go away. Yeah right, because that had worked *sooo* well that morning.

Then I was mad at Jarom. If I hadn't had to hold his hand at school, I never would have run to the car and my leg would be just fine. Then I was mad at myself for running to the stupid car in the first place. It wasn't fair! I had put in six solid months of training and one five-minute mistake could ruin it all.

While we were driving around working our way to Old Faithful, I entered the third phase, I started to pray. The Lord and I had been on better terms recently since I had been changing my life. I'd even been a Sunday church regular lately. I figured that God owed me one (dangerous thought to have, never ends well). I prayed and prayed for God to please heal my leg. I had read many other accounts of miracles and people being healed by the laying of hands. This was just a silly old tear in the hamstring, and surely the Lord could manage fixing that. I broached the subject with Jarom, but since he was a man of science, he didn't put too much stock in faith.

"You're more than welcome to try, but I wouldn't pin my hopes on it. The only thing you can do is stay off it and see where you are in two weeks."

I closed my eyes and prayed more. I got the distinct impression that the answer was no. My eyes started leaking around the edges again.

"Do you think I'll be able to run?" I asked quietly.

"I don't know, sweetheart."

"What do you think, though?"

Jarom considered for a moment. Probably trying to figure out whether to tell the truth or try to give me hope. He opted for the truth. "No, if it's what we think it is, then I don't think you'll be better in two weeks. I think you'll have to try again next year."

Slow trickles turned to steady streams. I tried to stay quiet, since the kids in the backseat were both engrossed in the movie playing. But I was crushed. Just the week before, I had been ready to run the whole marathon; but if the race had been today I would have been carted off the course before the first quarter mile. What was the point in being a finisher when life threw roadblocks in your way? I wanted to finish, but life didn't seem to want to let me. Everything I had worked hard for that year centered on completing the race. Without it, I would be nothing. The whole year wasted. Try again next year? Not likely. Not when I could make it so close and be thrown a curveball at the last minute.

I allowed myself the rest of the day to wallow in the depression stage. That night I lay in bed and prayed with earnest and openness, ready to hear what the Lord's reply would be. I had to be on my back since I currently couldn't bend at the knee without flexing the hamstring and crying out in pain. Last time I had basically commanded God to fix me; this time I laid bare my soul and asked for help.

"Please, Lord, this is very important to me. Is there anything I can do? Should I go to a doctor? If I have enough faith will I be healed? Tell me what to do."

I waited for an answer or a sign, or perhaps for a little relief of pain. None came, and that was probably an answer in itself. After the perfect eighteen-miler last week, I had envisioned my marathon going the same way. I needed to let that dream go, because there was no way that was going to happen now. I would even settle for walking the marathon, but if today was any indication that too seemed iffy at best. I had the feeling I was not receiving an answer because I was asking for the wrong thing.

"If my leg can't be healed, then please heal my heart, Father, because it is broken. Soothe my soul and help me to deal with my disappointment. Please help me to feel that my best is enough and accept whatever I can do."

Before I got to the "Amen," a warmth spread through my body. I had finally asked for the right blessing. I had the firm impression that no matter what happened, I was going to be okay, and he would make it okay. He wasn't going to fix me so I could run my dream marathon, but he would help me feel okay if I couldn't. Calm for the first time since the injury, sleep quickly overtook me.

***

When we got home, my leg had improved some, but stairs still took four times as long and I needed a handful of ibuprofen afterward. I took Jarom's approach to tapering and laid off the running altogether, skipping the final two weeks' worth of runs. Even though the odds were not in my favor, I wanted to give myself the best chance at success. I sought the opinion of sports trainers at the gym, a physical therapist, and a massage therapist. They all said the same thing: one, it was a moderate hamstring strain and, two, there was a good chance that if I ran the marathon, I would injure it further and put myself out of commission for months.

I didn't particularly like what I was hearing, so I opted to ignore. If I hurt myself further so what? This was not a training run, this was the real thing. I didn't need to be able to run after next Saturday, so if I was laid up for a few months and unable to exercise, I could deal. A decision needed to be made and only I could make it.

The Park City Marathon started officially at six thirty in the morning. Along the route there were two checkpoints that a runner had to clear by certain times to ensure that they finished the course in the allotted time. The organizers had thoughtfully provided an earlier start time at 5:00 a.m. for race walkers, allowing an extra hour and a half to reach the checkpoints. If I was going to have a snowball's chance in Hades, that was the only way. I needed to give myself every opportunity and advantage that I could.

Two days before the race, I was still technically a question mark on whether to attend. A quick mile run would help me make my final decision. If it went well, I would show up on race day at the earlier start time with Jarom at my side. If I couldn't manage the mile, then I would go with Jarom and cheer from the sidelines. For the past two weeks I had been doing everything physically possible to encourage healing: rest, ice, heat, compression, you name it. And it seemed to pay off. I completed a mile run at a slow jog without too much discomfort.

It would have been so easy to just say, "Hey I'm injured. I've got a doctor's note to prove it. It's not really quitting." I wasn't concerned in the slightest what anyone else would say. I'm sure no one would have faulted me for being cautious and passing on the race. But I knew that I would beat myself up for the rest of eternity wondering what if. Wondering what would have happened and how far I could've gone.

I personally can't stand a cliffhanger, so I opted to drag my butt to the start line and the inhumane hour of 5:00 a.m. There was a good chance that I wouldn't be able to finish, but at least I would be able to say that I tried. And I would keep trying, keep moving forward until I couldn't anymore. Then I'd drag myself a little farther until they carted me off the course.

I had made a commitment to this endeavor, and while life had stepped in and put an obstacle in my way, I was going to find a way around it. I might not make the whole twenty-six point two miles, but that was better than not starting at all. I needed to tweak my goal once again, but just a little. Sure I wanted to finish, but I would not do that at the expense of my health. My new goal was to get to the starting line, participate in a marathon, and see how far my bum leg would carry me. And whatever the outcome, as long as I gave every ounce that I had, it would be enough.

15

YOU CAN *do* HARD THINGS

On August 20, ten months after the thud, Jarom and I woke up at 4:30 a.m. and got ready for the biggest, scariest event of our lives—aside from becoming parents, that is. The night before, I had pinned the racing bib on my shirt so the number 346 was proudly displayed. I'd also pre-packed my waist belt with water, energy gel, anti-inflammatory pain medicine, and an ACE bandage. Of course I hoped my leg held up, but I wanted to be prepared just in case.

We lined up with the other penguins at the starting line just before 5:00 . . . in the dark. Fortunately we had thought to bring headlamps so we could see where we were running. The race official welcomed us and gave us a few course warnings. The course wasn't closed, so we needed to watch for traffic. Also, since it was so early, the aid stations weren't set up yet, so we were on our own. And as a last piece of advice: don't get lost. It was predawn and dark, and there was a turn somewhere around mile four that people often missed.

My stomach was already in knots of nervousness, but the thought of getting lost and running in the wrong direction made me want to hurl my morning bagel. I was terrified that with my poor vision in particular, that I would miss the arrow on the pavement and keep going straight. My heart was palpitating and my breathing was erratic.

I turned around to go back to the hotel, but Jarom wouldn't let me. He said, "Ha ha, very funny," like I was just being silly. I'm not so sure. Part of me was definitely being dramatic and funny, but the other half was scared to death. I have a phobia of being lost from way back when I was a kid and my parents lost me in the Seattle-Tacoma airport. They were through the plane gate before they realized I was missing. I envisioned running off miles away from the course, in some random neighborhood. Jarom promised that he would make sure I didn't get lost, and if we both missed the turn, then at least we would be together. Somehow that wasn't as comforting as he intended it to be. While I had been freaking out, the race official had positioned everyone at the start. It was time to go.

There was no gunshot in the air, no crowd cheering, and thankfully no large throng of sardines. Just a man saying "good luck," and then twenty people with flashlights and headlamps started their twenty-six-point-two-mile trek. There were a couple of solitary runners that took off pretty fast, but most of us were cloistered in small groups, joking and jogging casually.

Jarom and I started out at a fairly slow pace, even for us. We wanted to make sure to not push our injuries before the muscles had warmed up. Even at our slower start, within a mile we were at the front of the small pack, only three others ahead of us. Well, wasn't that a change. Soon we were by ourselves with only the streetlights for company. It was so quiet and reverent that I couldn't bring myself to break the spell with my headphones. So Jarom and I whispered back and forth to each other.

"Are we going the right way?"

"Yes, I saw an arrow just a minute ago."

"Are you sure?"

"Yes, but you can go back and check if you want."

"No, no I trust you. I can't see a thing."

"I know."

Pause

"How's your leg?" he asked.

I considered for a minute and took brief mental stock of my physical condition.

"Surprisingly well. And your calf?"

"Hasn't bugged me yet."

"Good, I'm glad. As long as we keep going the right way, I think we'll finish."

"I hope so."

"Which? That we're going the right way or that we'll finish?"

"Both."

And that was how we passed the first four and a half miles. As we approached the tricky turn, the morning sky began to bleed hues of pink into the void of black. It was a good thing the official had warned us ahead of time, because we would have missed it. You literally turned up someone's driveway and next to their backyard to get to the bridge that helped you cross under the highway. One of the front-runners had missed it, because as we turned he came running back down the road from the opposite direction. "Oops," he said as he passed us, earning a few chuckles in return.

As soon as we crossed under the overpass, the tension left my body. The dawn was beautiful, the world was still, and we felt as if were the only creatures on earth. The next few miles were magic, like Disney happily ever after magic. I've always enjoyed the benefits of running, both physical and mental, but I never actually enjoyed it while I was running. Sarah Michelle always said, "Isn't it addicting? I just love the runner's high." My reply was that you had to be high to love running. Now I got it. I was in the zone and loved every step I took, knowing each one was taking me closer to the finish line.

Around mile eight, my leg muscles started twitching. I had been running for an hour and a half, so I reasoned that my leg must be getting a little tight. For the next mile, I backed off the pace a little bit but still said nothing to my running partner. By mile nine my hamstring felt like it was ripping itself in two. I grabbed Jarom's arm and pulled him to the side.

"My leg is killing me. I'm going stop and try wrapping it and see if that helps."

So I wrapped it and jogged a half-mile. It was better but still painful to run on. So I tried rewrapping it, trying to isolate the right muscles and bind them tight. For the next two miles I jogged, walked then stopped to reposition, run, walk and stop, and so on. It stopped getting better; it only got worse. Jarom's watch beeping held no meaning for me anymore. I could only run for thirty seconds at time before the pain became unbearable. I was so screwed.

At mile twelve I knew that running was no longer an option. After only a few steps of running the pain was rending and excruciating, causing me to stop and rest for a minute by the side of the road. Well, now what? I wasn't tired. I had the energy to keep going, but my leg said, "Uh-uh, no more." I'd known from previous runs that stopping cools your muscles and that was a bad idea for me right now. So between miles twelve and thirteen I walked and pondered. What did I have to lose if I kept going? I wanted that stained-glass finisher medal, and I wasn't going to get it if I gave up now.

It occurred to me that I hadn't had to stop in pain recently, since I began walking in fact. Was it fixed? I hopped a little to confirm. Pain. Nope, not fixed. Okay then, running, jogging, or any skipping-like gait took my breath away it hurt so bad. Walking leisurely or even power walking, as long as I didn't pick my leg up too high or bend the knee, was fine. Okay, that's a lie. It wasn't fine, and it still hurt like a son of a biscuit, but it was better. It was doable, and that's all that I needed.

Jarom was a champ, sticking with me through the first thirteen miles, a half marathon's worth. Our time for the first eight miles had been on target, but the last five had gotten progressively slower. I was going to give everything I had to get to the end, but I didn't know realistically if that would be enough. Or how long it would take me. Jarom's leg, on the other hand, was doing great, and he had an excellent chance at finishing the race, but only if he could clear the checkpoints in time.

"You need to go."

"What do you mean?"

"I can't run anymore. There is just no possible way, so I'm going to race-walk. But I have no idea how slow that'll be. So you go on ahead and get past the checkpoints in time, and I'll meet you at the finish, okay?"

Jarom looked at me dubiously. "Are you sure? You'll be okay?"

"Yep, I'll be fine. We've both got our phones, so I'll text you if I get stuck."

"Okay, I'll text every couple miles and see where you are and how you're doing." He kissed my sweaty head and resumed Jarom speed.

Most of me was happy to see him go. This had started out as his dream, and I didn't want to be a hindrance to his completion. I mean how awful would I feel if my slower pace made him too late, missing the allotted time to reach the checkpoint at miles seventeen and twenty? Honestly, only about 10 percent of me was staring at his back indignant in unbelief that he actually took off without me.

Not too long after Jarom left, a man flew by me. This was most likely the eventual marathon winner. I'd had an hour and a half head start, and around mile fourteen, he had caught up. As he whizzed by, I clapped and whistled encouragingly. He smiled graciously and didn't miss a step; he couldn't because his competition was hot on his heels. It was pretty cool to see the fast runners in action. They were pretty amazing. Not too much later, the fastest female passed me. She was long and lean and actually waved at me as she passed my hooting and hollering.

I wanted to stop and get her autograph she was so awesome, but that was not really practical in the middle of a race. For a minute I had actually forgotten that, since I was going at such a leisurely pace. Not to mention I wasn't tired at all and was having fun. My phone shrilled at me, indicating I had a new text. Jarom was letting me know he was now at the first checkpoint a mile ahead. I checked my watch and realized that as long as kept the same pace, I too would reach the checkpoint in plenty of time. Well, hot dang, my race wasn't over just yet.

I picked up the pace and pushed myself faster until my leg protested, then I eased off a little bit. My own fancy watch said my pace was averaging fourteen-and-a-half-minute miles. Not too shabby for walking. I did some quick math and realized that as long as I kept going, I was going to make it; I was going to finish a marathon.

The first checkpoint was at the ski resort, and one of the first real challenging aspects of the course, a steep incline. Halfway up the hill, Jarom texted his progress again, and I texted back that I was almost at the checkpoint. He seemed a little surprised that I hadn't fallen further behind. I admit I felt a little bit of competition. It was blatantly obvious that Jarom was going to beat me, but I was going to narrow that gap any way I could. On the way back down the incline from the ski lodge, I had the brilliant idea to see if I could run briefly on this quarter-mile stretch of downhill. Stupid, but my leg was feeling so much better, I thought it might be worth it to try again. The only thing I accomplished was maybe gaining ten seconds and making my leg sore all over again.

My renewed pain made the next mile stretch the most difficult of the whole marathon, it was mile eighteen. When I passed that mile marker, I realized that this was the furthest I had ever run (walked, limped . . . whatever) in my life. I hit a wall. Not literally this time, just figuratively. People were now passing me left and right, and it was a little hard to be left behind. There were eight miles left, and I wasn't sure I had them in me.

Running over a wooden bridge, I saw a little girl on the sidelines, ringing a cowbell and holding a sign for her mom. She was a little blondie just like my girls. When I passed her, she waved and smiled and rang her cowbell for me. Tears ran down my face of their own accord. Lily and Autumn were at home with Grandpa, but I imagined they were here watching me and cheering me on. As I passed other people, they too shouted encouragement and clapped, and I'm sure I looked like an idiot, walking as fast as I could, crying. I smiled through my tears and kept moving, never breaking stride. I'm pretty sure if I stopped, even for a second, I would not be able to get going again.

It was getting harder to continue, and my chest was tight from trying to keep from crying. I didn't know what the tears were about. I was happy and touched by the crowd's support. I was also overwhelmed and in pain. Before I knew it, I could see the bigger steep hill ahead, the reason this course was labeled as difficult. What if I couldn't climb it or had to stop because my leg stalled out? It looked really hard. At the base of the hill, next to the arrow, was a frowny face spray painted on the pavement. Good to know it wasn't just me that didn't like this part. Looking up, I could see lots of runners that had breezed by me not too long ago leaning over and panting. As far as I could see, not a single person was running up the hill; they were all walking or hiking.

To psych myself up, I remembered our new family motto, "You can do hard things." It came from Lily's occupational therapist. When Lily didn't want to do one of her exercises for her nervous system, she always said, "Nope, it's too hard," and her OT would reply, "Well, guess what, Lily? You are SuperLily, and you can do hard things." And so it became the family motto since we said it so often to her. Being hard wasn't a good enough excuse to run away, because I was SuperBetsy, and I could do hard things.

And so I trudged onward and upward. At the halfway point up the hill, there was a spray painted face with a squiggly mouth, almost like a grimace. It made me laugh, but not as hard as the one at the top. Next to the arrow pointing to the left was the biggest smile and crinkly eyes spray-painted on a happy face that I had ever seen. It was accurate too, since the expression was duplicated on every single runner's face as they crested over the top.

I texted Jarom to let him know I had made it over the top. He texted back that he was glad because that almost killed him. It was pretty much literally downhill from there, in a good way. The hardest part was over, and I was once again confident that I could finish. Without the worry, I began to really enjoy the race and the beautiful scenery. People would pass me and shout, "Keep going!" or "You can do it!" as they ran by. At crosswalks, the traffic officers commented as well, one saying, "Great pace. Keep it up. Four miles to go."

Around mile twenty-three, I saw a runner stop and sit at the aid station. She loudly exclaimed to her companions, "That's it! I can't go another step." She took off her running shoes and massaged her feet. One of her toenails looked kinda mangled. How sad it was to be within three miles and give up. Come on, you've already run twenty-three, what's a few more? I had to keep my forward momentum going, or else I would share the same fate. Still, I thought about her as I walked the next mile. I imagined she had built up the remaining sliver of the race as an impossible feat, instead of seeing all that she had already done. I really hoped that she changed her mind, put her shoe back on, and kept going. But if she did, she never passed me.

With less than two miles to the finish line, Jarom texted me that he was done, that he had finished the marathon. I was so proud of him. I texted my position and that I'd see him in a few. After I put my phone away, I noticed that I was about to pass a portly man in a Day-Glo yellow running shirt. We had been playing leapfrog for the last few miles or so; he would run ahead and pass me, then slow to a crawl and take a break. Since I was keeping a steady pace, I would pass him, and then seven minutes later or so he would pass me again. Apparently it was my turn again, but this time he looked pretty bad off. He stopped to lean on the fence and appeared beat. I yelled out as I approached him.

"Are you doing okay? Do you need a gel? I've got some extra if you need it."

"No, thanks, I've got some too. I'm just tired and my legs are jelly."

"Walk with me, because I can't stop. Just keep moving, and you'll get there eventually."

He chuckled and probably thought I was nuts, but he got in step with me anyway. Maybe it hurt his pride to have a girl walking beat him; maybe he just needed a little encouragement. Don't know. We chatted for a minute, and he asked about my funny stiff walk. I told him about my leg and he was shocked that I'd shown up at all. Yep, me too. Before he took off running again, I offered up a little bit of encouragement, just like others had been doing for me.

"You know, it feels like the last two miles are the hardest, but think about the first twenty-four. You got through those, so I know you can get through these too."

"Thank you. Good luck and God bless."

What a nice man. I never asked his name, so I couldn't look up the race results later. But I think he finished, because over those last two miles, I never passed him again.

Toward the end, I could hear the crowd and the announcer calling names as they crossed the finish line. This had definitely not been the marathon of my dreams. I hadn't been able to run the whole thing. I wasn't even able to do the timed run/walk thing. My time wasn't anywhere near the five hours fifteen minutes I had projected before my injury. Jarom was not by my side. There was one thing though that would be the same. I was going to finish. And by golly, I would finish running. I waited to start running until I rounded the corner on the home stretch, and for the last two tenths of a mile, I ran.

I crossed the finish line, sobbing from pain and relief. The medical workers asked me if I was okay since I was limping and crying so hard. Nodding that I was, since words were beyond my ability at that time, I shuffled forward to get my reward: the stained-glass finisher medal. A young woman hung it around my neck and gave me a carnation, and at the same time I saw Jarom. I launched myself at him and sobbed even harder. We had done it. We had done the impossible. We had proved absolutely that we could do hard things. For a few moments we held each other, cried, and let it all out.

It was one of the best moments of my life, right up there with saying "I do" and looking into my girls' eyes for the first time. By running the marathon I had done what I had set out to do—to prove that no task is too hard or too big to try. Because, if I could run a marathon, then I could do anything.

And I did, so that meant that I could.

16

the *BEST* INTROSPECTION COMES WHEN YOU THINK YOU'RE GOING *to* DIE

I f a fortune teller would have predicted, on the morning of the thud, that in ten months I was going to finish a marathon, I would have windexed her crystal ball and asked for my money back. But here I was—a marathoner. (I love the sound of that.)

Jarom had finished twenty-one minutes ahead of me, in 5:45:00. I finished in 6:06:00. Not a stellar time, but still faster than the runners that didn't finish. My entire family was pretty surprised I had made it, and, to be honest, I was a little surprised too. It's one thing to tell yourself that you're going to do something, but it's quite another when you actually do. So where was the ticker tape parade and the marching band? I gave myself one in my head, because I had earned it. My daughters wanted to play with my "pretty new necklace." Not a chance; they would have to pry this medal out of my cold, dead hands.

We spent the rest of the day celebrating, and food never tasted so good. I ate whatever I wanted since I had just burned off a whopping 3,000 calories. Like I've said before, dessert tastes better without the side of guilt. The satisfaction of completing our goal was unlike anything I had ever felt. I went to bed with an extremely sore leg and a sore face from smiling all day long.

The next day I wasn't smiling much anymore. My parents were excited that the race was over because now they wouldn't have to watch the girls for two-hour runs anymore or be subjected to endless discussions about running. But I was sad. It's like looking forward to Christmas, then the holiday letdown on December 26, when it's over. My adventure was over, and I was once again left without a purpose. I resumed my position in the recliner and began working on making a new smaller bum indentation.

One day back in my old chair convinced me that I needed to find a new adventure. How had I ever stood mindless hours on this thing? A stack of good books helped, one of them being *Eat, Pray, Love*. I found that a little humorous since I had changed my life through the Starve, Whine, Dislike approach, or at least that's how it started off. But now I was happy with my life, my relationship with food, my relationship with God, and my relationship with exercise. It wasn't quite love, more like Eat, Pray, Tolerate. But still, I had turned myself into a finisher after being a lifelong quitter.

So why wasn't I out there, busy conquering the world? Mostly, I was focusing on trying to heal up my leg, the marathon had done a number on that left hamstring and knee. For two and a half solid weeks I hardly moved from the chair except to get more ice and new bandages. I was pulling my hair out from the cabin fever, and that's the only excuse I have for agreeing to climb a mountain. I needed to get out and do something, anything. So when our friends the Becks asked Jarom and me to go hiking with them on Labor Day, I quickly committed without thinking it through. After all, wouldn't reaching the pinnacle of a tall mountain finish off my yearlong adventure perfectly?

The day before the hike, I began to get cold feet. My back window had the perfect view of the mountain we were going to climb, Lone Peak. It looked really, really high. I don't do too well with high. Looking from the base of the mountain to the tippy top and back down again, the visual did not compute. How was something like that even possible? It may as well have been Mount Everest as far as I was concerned. How on earth did someone get up into the clouds without either an airplane or a Sherpa and a donkey to carry you?

Jarom was downright giddy with excitement. I told you before that he was into all this kind of stuff. He had already climbed Lone Peak once and had climbed Mount Rainier in Washington many years ago, so he wasn't the least bit worried. This was his element, what he loved to do. He would be happy living the rest of his life in woods somewhere. Not so much with me. My family's idea of roughing it was staying at the Holiday Inn Express instead of the Hilton. Hiking and nature aren't something you do; they're something you watch on the Discovery Channel. I didn't know what to expect and none of my other outdoorsy attempts had ended well before.

"So, Jarom, realistically, how long is this hike?"

"Boy, it's been years and years, but if I remember right it should take us about six hours."

"And is it really hard, or is it something that even I can do?"

"Of course you can do it. You just ran a marathon. You can do anything."

I was so pleased at the answer that I failed to notice that he had skirted around the issue of difficulty. Since he hadn't expressly warned me, I assumed it was a casual hike, difficult because of the time involved rather than the terrain. Well, I had finished a marathon, so I figured I had plenty of endurance. I trusted Jarom, and if he believed that I could do it and be safe, then I would be fine.

***

Forty-five minutes into our ascent, I resolved to never trust Jarom again as long as I lived. It's my own darned fault for not getting more information before I agreed to this cockamamie stunt. You know what they say about what happens when you assume—it makes an (bleep) out of U and ME. Apparently that made me the donkey that was trekking up the mountain. The four of us took a break after an hour to munch on some trail mix. I looked up at the peak we were somehow magically supposed to reach. Jay Beck misinterpreted my disbelief for wonder. (The only wonder going on was wondering what on earth I was doing.)

"It's beautiful, isn't it?"

"Yes, it's pretty. But what would make anyone think 'Hey, look at that mountain over there, I think I should go climb that'?"

"Betsy, can't you hear it beckoning? Calling to you to stand on the top?"

I listened for just a moment. "Nope, no beckoning. Everything about it screams 'Stay away or die.'"

Everybody laughed, thinking that I was just making a joke, but I was serious. This was stupid and insane. I got a little panicked. What if my leg acted up again? Would I be stuck up here? Would little Mounties come and get me? I had lost weight, but I'm pretty sure I was still too heavy for Jarom to carry me down. For one minute, I felt an absolute certainty that I was going to die on this dumb mountain.

My hiking companions stood up and started climbing again. I seriously considered doing what I had always done before . . . quit. Two problems with that, though. For one, I didn't pack a book, and five hours would be a long time to wait by myself without anything to do except become mountain lion food. The other problem you probably already guessed: I had committed to do it, and I was a finisher and not a quitter. It would not bode well for the longevity of my life changes if I folded at the first post-marathon outing.

I took a moment to myself and said a quick prayer that I might survive this endeavor, then I began hiking with renewed intent. This would be just like the marathon, just like everything else I had done this year—only a lot harder and uphill. Climbing a mountain was the final exam to see if I could put all my new skills to use in my life. Seventy-five pounds sounded like a lot, but I did one pound at a time. And so far I had run nearly 500 miles, but it too started with just one. Looking up at the peak made my heart palpitate and gave me vertigo, so instead of focusing my energy worrying about how to make it to the top, I needed to focus on where to place my feet in front of me. As long as I kept climbing, I would get there eventually.

So I made small talk with my companions to keep my mind occupied and only joked occasionally asking, "Are we there yet?" All that mattered was climbing the little path that I could see in front of my feet. When I finished that one, I focused on the next little bit. We broke for lunch at four hours, and we were probably about two-thirds the way up the mountain.

"So am I just really slow? Because I don't think it's going to be possible to make it up the rest of the way and back down in two more hours."

Martha looked intrigued. "Why would you be able to do that?"

"Because Jarom told me it was about a six-hour hike."

"Oh no. That would be really fast. You'd have to run the whole way, I think."

I shot Jarom a dirty look. Somebody was sleeping with the dog tonight.

Jay asked Jarom, "Have you summited this one? Is that how long it took you?"

Jarom squirmed uncomfortably. "Well, it was about six years ago, so my memory is a little fuzzy. Now that I think about it, I never actually made it to the top. A lightning storm forced me to come back down."

To look at me, you would have thought I was trying to catch flies, my mouth was open so wide. I had been duped, tricked, bamboozled. Surely I could not be held accountable to finish an activity I was led to under false pretenses. Probably not, but what could I do about it now? I was already most of the way up, and to turn around and go home without finishing would have been just as bad as the marathon lady with the mangled toenail.

That didn't save Jarom from my scathing looks that promised retribution. It did not go unnoticed either that he quickly finished his lunch and went to the front to hike with Jay. Humph, good thing I knew where he lived.

I forced my feet to continue forward, and make no mistake, it was forced. During the marathon, I had found pockets of magic and generally had fun. This was just miserable. I didn't enjoy the arduous hiking over granite, didn't like tripping over it either. For the most part I kept my opinions to myself. After all, I was a guest on this hike and didn't want to sound like an obnoxious brat full of whiny complaints. My mind stayed busy thinking of all the things I would make Jarom do when we got home. He owed me big time, and I was keeping score with every stumble.

The last bit before the peak was no longer hiking; it was true climbing. As in scrambling up and around huge slabs of granite bigger than my car . . . without ropes. Go figure that the spot with most danger and biggest chance of actual dying, was the only time I had fun. All my yoga and strength training was paying off, because I was easily surpassing the rest of the group with my increased flexibility and arm strength. I was able to take shortcuts that Jarom couldn't because I could get my leg much higher on the rock.

And then we were there, the top of the world. Or at least the top of mine. According to Wikipedia, Lone Peak is 11,253 feet in elevation and usually requires one to two days for this difficult hike. (Why didn't I think to look up that info before?!) The view was breathtaking. I couldn't pick out the tiny speck that was my house from here, but I knew that the view from my back window was forever altered. Now I could look out and see Lone Peak and picture me standing on top. Getting here had sucked, but it was still so worth it. I wanted to jump up and down, but given the precarious nature of the highest rock, I decided that was a bad idea. The four of us took pictures, and I forgave Jarom for tricking me and let him pose next to me. Had I known what lay in store for me, I never would have come. But now I was really glad that I had.

Jarom had been semi correct, as in it took us nearly six hours to reach the peak. It's not fair that we spent that much time to get there and only got to spend ten minutes at the top before heading back. And therein lies the problem inherent in mountain climbing. I had reached the top, finished my goal, and I was done and ready to go home. But now I had to do it all over again, in reverse. It's like running a marathon, crossing the finish line, and then running back to the start to pick up your car. Whoever said its easier going downhill than uphill lied. Or at least that was the case for me. My hamstring and knee really did not like going down. I think it was a combination of the angle and trying to control my descent so I wasn't racing down or tumbling down end over end.

It was my personal hell. I was afraid of falling since I had so much experience with it. Most other hikes Jarom had forced me on, I had scooted down on my bum and ripped my pants open, but I really liked these pants, and I was much farther up that I had ever been before. There was no guarantee that once I started sliding I would stop. Every time that I lost my footing and slid down a few feet, my heart would pound, and tears would well in my eyes. The others were little mountain goats and far ahead of me. Jarom, more often than not, would come back and check on me, but on the return trip I was largely alone.

To chase away the thoughts of crashing to the jagged rocks below, I thought about what an awesome year I'd had. I'd gone from a big fat nobody, to smaller somebody, to realizing I had been a somebody all along, even if it was a fat somebody. My life was so much better. A year ago I didn't believe I was capable of doing anything, and look at me now. I had climbed one of the tallest mountains on the Wasatch Front. Now I just needed to survive getting down.

The old me would have been concerned about how long I was taking, as in much longer than the rest of my group. I would have beat myself up and felt bad for holding them up. Then I would have attempted to go faster and probably fallen and broken something in the process. New me realized that I didn't have to worry about anyone but me. I was doing the best that I could to ensure I finished safely and that was enough.

I was technically the same person as I was a year ago, my DNA hadn't changed, but the way I viewed the world and my place in it had. No longer did I see the world in black and white, looking for perfection and then spiraling into a depression when I didn't find it. I didn't need to be the best anymore; I just needed to finish. I will most likely never win a race, but that fact shouldn't stop me from running it anyway.

And that's when everything I had learned came together into one sentence. I like to call it my Philosophy of Finishing: Not everyone can win the race, but everyone can finish it. Never again would I quit because I was afraid of what the world—or my little voice—might say. I could look fear in the eye and point to the mountain of finishes that was building up in the back of my mind and yell, "I can do it! I'm awesome!"

Eleven hours (six hours my foot) and one black toenail (downward pressure pushes on the nail, causing it to injure and fall off) after I started up the rocky path, I returned to the car. I'm not sure which I was more proud of honestly—making it the top or making it back down with my pants intact. Either way, I had another hard task under my belt. No one was at the car to give me a finisher medal this time. But I gave one to myself. It's the mental image of Jarom's face at the top of the mountain. He was so proud that, for the first time, I had actually made it all the way to the top with him. That I was able to share something that meant so much to him was all the reward I needed. Well, maybe a hot bath too.

EPILOGUE

the PHILOSOPHY *of* FINISHING

There was no "now what?" moment or letdown the next day (although my toenail did fall off) because the hike down had given me the direction that I was going to take for the rest of my life. I officially had a new way of living. I was no longer a follower of the Path of Whatever is Easiest, but I was a subscriber to the Philosophy of Finishing. Heck, I was the charter member. But I wasn't going to live it alone. The more I shared my stories with friends and family, the more my little lessons started seeping into their lives as well. By the time we ran the marathon, the conversion had already begun.

Naturally Jarom was the first aside from me to start living the Principles of Finishing. I had mentioned earlier that Jarom was going back to school. What I didn't elaborate on was that he was going back to college at the age of thirty-five after a ten-year sabbatical. Not finishing a degree was one of Jarom's greatest regrets in life. For the past nine years or so we had discussed the possibility of him going back, but he would always inevitably decide that with a full-time job and now kids, there just wasn't enough time. Then there was coming up with tuition. It would be too hard. He would have to take night classes and then only a few a semester. It would take forever. And of course the longer the "break" from school lasted, the more difficult it was to see himself amongst the other, younger students.

But this time, when the semiannual discussion about whether or not he should enroll that semester came up about a month prior to the marathon, it went a little differently. Instead of starting with "I'd really like to get my degree, but I just don't think it's really plausible," now he said to me, "I want to get my degree. Will you help me figure out to do that?" Hallelujah, he had seen the light. So after the kids went to sleep, we sat down and discussed the logistics and what we were realistically looking at. All the obstacles from previous discussions were there plus a few more. With the economy and the job market in its current state, we were making less than before, working longer hours, and had less job security to boot. But this was something that was really important to him. This was his thud moment. He had never been fat, but he could no longer live with the weight of the unfinished degree hanging over his head. Using everything we had learned recently, we made a plan to make it work. This was not going to be a one and done kind of thing. Working around a fulltime job meant a few classes at a time, lasting probably six semesters. But Jarom and I were now the masters of finishing hard things at a slow pace. As long as he kept checking those classes off the required to graduate list, he would earn his degree eventually. And he would get it faster than if never went back at all.

He is going to get his degree, and we decided together that we wouldn't let anything stand in the way of that. Paying for tuition and books meant taking a long hard look at how much those extra cable channels and dinners out were worth. But the money just wasn't a good enough excuse to keep him from what he wants to do. There is never a good excuse to keep you from what you really want, is there? And Jarom decided he really wanted it. He signed up for the classes he could fit into his schedule, met with his (younger than him) academic advisor, and started attending classes.

It certainly wasn't easy for him. He struggled with his old nemesis—procrastination. And he fights a battle with social anxiety disorder every time he has to go to campus.

But he does it. Because he can do hard things. And I am happy to report that at the end of 2011 he got an associate of science degree, and now he's pressing on for his bachelor's degree in biology.

Sometimes it can be difficult to see the change in ourselves, but I am amazed daily at the positive changes I can see in my family. I am starting early with my kids and teaching them that they need to finish what they start. While that can sometimes be difficult with the attention span of a four-year-old and two-year-old, they are getting it. It's really nice on the everyday little things because they know that if a toy comes out to play, you're not done playing until it goes back in the toy chest. That makes my formerly frequently stubbed toes very happy.

Autumn is too little to grasp the finer points of finishing, but I think Lily has without really meaning too. All I used to hear out of that little preschooler was "I can't do it. It's too hard. I'm not any good at it." But now that she is working on finishing, there's a little hill of proof in the back of her mind too. When she starts to get anxious about something, I remind her of all the things she's done and that whatever it is we are attempting will be a piece of cake because she's SuperLily. It's like a veil lifting from her eyes; you can see the light go on and the wheels turn and all of a sudden she's not afraid to try any more.

Before the thud, my marriage wasn't bad, but it's certainly better now. I'm sure Jarom would never say this (out loud) but I think it has helped not having to hear me sob every time I hop on the scale. Or listen to me complain about what I can't eat. Or worry about coming up with the right answer to the age-old question, "Does this make me look fat?" I think we are happier as a couple because finishing has made us happier as individuals. He no longer beats himself up about the unfinished kitchen since one of the things he's learned is that he can only do so much at once. And for him that's keeping a steady job, finishing school, and being a good husband and father. And then, most important, letting the things that aren't at the top of the list go for now. A big part of finishing is picking the right goal and focusing on that.

That's something I learned too. My to-do list is long. It looks a little something like this.

1. **Write book**

2. **Potty train Autumn**

3. **Organize entire house**

4. **Run marathon uninjured**

5. **Climb the highest peaks in every county in Utah (Jarom's idea obviously)**

6. Sew fat clothes quilt with minimal amount of blood loss

7. Learn to cook without burning the house down (that one may very well be impossible . . . we'll see)

8. Get a bachelor's degree

9. Start playing piano again

10. Learn to play bass guitar

Now if I try to do all those things by next year, I would probably fail miserably. For everything there is a season, and my calendar says it's not time for a lot of those. So I picked the ones that are really important to me, such as one and two—because I am *sooo* done with poopy diapers— and focus my energies on those.

But a big part of the Philosophy of Finishing is in the little every-day details. After all, you can't do huge life-altering things everyday, can you? That would be exhausting. But I take all the lightbulb lessons I've learned and use them in my day-to-day life. I make sure the girls and I finish something every day. (If Lily has her way, it usually involves paint and sparkles.) I stopped estimating the waist size (and bra size) of the girl standing next to me in the checkout line. Old photos don't make me want to cry anymore, and I can pass by the mirror without tossing my hairbrush at it.

I don't yell at myself anymore on the days where it's all I can do to get the kids safely though the day without throttling them. Now that I am in control of my life, I can decide which days I need to go slow and which days I can do it all. Fear doesn't own me now. I'm not afraid of some big cosmic smackdown coming to knock me off my course. If an obstacle pops up in my way, I know I'll find a way around it, over it, or dig a freak-ing tunnel under it if I have to. Whatever it takes to finish.

Or however long it takes. Because I might not be the fastest or the best at everything I do, but that is not going to stop me anymore. I will not bury my talents (parable of the talents) just because they might not be as big or bright as someone else's. I will not cut my efforts short just because it's apparent that I won't win. Everything is worth finishing. And as long as I do the best I can and give all that I am, then I will be success-ful in whatever I do—regardless of how I stack up against anyone else.

Let's be honest. Sometimes the electricity goes out in my brain, or that little epiphany lightbulb burns out for a minute. I cannot be perfect. I can't even live my own philosophy perfectly. I'm going to make mistakes, and that's okay. Because I am in the driver's seat, I will take responsibility for that, then choose to initiate that little spark of correction or put in a new lightbulb. But my faults are not the end of the world, and I don't have to beat myself up about them. The sun will come out tomorrow and all that jazz.

I'm not ashamed of who I am anymore. I am a collector of finisher medals. Some are going to be real, because even as I'm writing this, I have begun training for another marathon. (I think it's like childbirth; after a little time you forget the pain of labor or, in this case, training.) Others will be symbolic like the necklace my sister gave me. It is the symbol that I survived a very tough time with my daughter. Then there are the medals I create in my mind that stand for all the other things I do. These are the ones that keep stacking up, building a mountain inside of me—the mountain that I stand on and look at the world and its possibilities. It's getting so high I can barely see the wall of failures I had built below.

free
OFFER!

Want to lose weight? Sometimes the hardest part is having a clue where to begin. The bulk of my weight came off and stayed off because I learned to stick to a budget. Not a grocery budget, but a calorie budget. If I overspent my calories, I would get fat and inflated just like the nation's national debt. Find your daily budget and underspend.

Have no idea how much you should be spending? That's where this offer comes in. I'm truly committed to helping people make a lifestyle change and learn how to budget so they never have to go on a "diet" ever again. If you go to my website, www.betsyschow.com, click on the offers page and fill out the form, I'll work up a personalized calorie budget for you. Once you know what your budget is, you can learn to live within your caloric means.

Part of the budget is fitting in exercise. Why not start with yoga? It strengthens the mind and the body. I fell in love with it and became certified so I could teach it to people of every level of fitness. With your budget I will also include a yoga routine you can do at home.

LET ME HELP YOU GET STARTED TOWARD YOUR FINISH LINE!

READY . . . SET . . . GO!

Betsy Schow